GOSPEL HOUR
SERMONS

GOSPEL HOUR SERMONS

by

Oliver B. Greene

BAKER BOOK HOUSE

Grand Rapids, Michigan

Library of Congress Catalog Card Number: 63-20013

First printing, January 1963—10,000 copies
Second printing, July 1964—10,000 copies
Third printing, June 1965—10,000 copies
Fourth printing, July 1968—15,000 copies
Fifth printing, January 1972—15,000 copies
Sixth printing, November 1973—15,000 copies

$4.00

Copyright 1963, by
BAKER BOOK HOUSE COMPANY

Contents

Rocks, Rags, and Leaves

Chapter I

Rocks, Rags, and Leaves

"Enter ye in at the strait gate: for wide is the gate, and broad is the way, that leadeth to destruction, and many there be which go in thereat: Because strait is the gate, and narrow is the way, which leadeth unto life, and few there be that find it. Beware of false prophets, which come to you in sheep's clothing, but inwardly they are ravening wolves. Ye shall know them by their fruits. Do men gather grapes of thorns, or figs of thistles? Even so every good tree bringeth forth good fruit; but a corrupt tree bringeth forth evil fruit. A good tree cannot bring forth evil fruit, neither can a corrupt tree bring forth good fruit. Every tree that bringeth not forth good fruit is hewn down, and cast into the fire. Wherefore by their fruits ye shall know them. Not everyone that saith unto me, Lord, Lord, shall enter into the kingdom of heaven; but he that doeth the will of my Father which is in heaven. Many will say to me in that day, Lord, Lord, have we not prophesied in thy name? and in thy name have cast out devils? and in thy name done many wonderful works? And then will I profess unto them, I never knew you: depart from me, ye that work iniquity. Therefore whosoever heareth these sayings of mine, and doeth them, I will liken him unto a wise man, which built his house upon a rock: and the rain descended, and the floods came, and the winds blew, and beat upon that house; and it fell not: for it was founded upon a rock. And every one that heareth these sayings of mine, and doeth them not, shall be likened unto a foolish man, which built his house upon the sand: and the rain descended, and the floods came, and the winds blew, and beat upon that house; and it fell: and great was the fall of it. And it came to pass, when Jesus had ended these sayings, the people were astonished at his doctrine: for he taught them as one having authority, and not as the scribes" (Matthew 7:13-29).

The Sermon on the Mount closes with admonition and solemn warning. We are admonished to *enter in at the strait gate*. The way to destruction is broad — and many travel that way; but the way of life eternal is straight and narrow — and "few there be that find it." Jesus made no mistake when He said, "Many are called, but few are chosen" (Matt. 22:14).

That does not mean that only a few are chosen to be saved. Many are called — but only a few choose to be saved.

"Beware of false prophets!" is the solemn warning sounded out in the closing verses of the marvelous Sermon on the Mount. One of the signs of the end is false prophets, of which we have many today. New religions and cults are springing up daily. Beware of these!

In this Scripture Jesus also warns of the danger of profession without possession — "religion" without saving faith. Not all who say, "Lord, Lord," shall enter into the beautiful city foursquare — but only those who do the will of God. The will of God is clearly defined in John 6:40: "And this is the will of him that sent me, that every one which seeth the Son, and believeth on him, may have everlasting life: and I will raise him up at the last day."

It is the will of God that we believe on His Son, Jesus Christ — the Son who finished the work the Father sent Him to do; the Son about whom the Father said, "I am well pleased"; the Son who is the Door, the Way, the Truth, the Life; the Son who said, "No man cometh to the Father but by me!" (John 14:6). According to Matthew 7:21-23, a great multitude who thought they were going to enter the kingdom of Heaven, will enter the lake of fire instead. They will be those who depend upon good works instead of doing the will of God — namely, believing on the Lord Jesus Christ and trusting Him as personal Saviour.

The last few verses in the Sermon on the Mount describe two builders. No one could miss the meaning of the illustration Jesus gives here, unless he does so deliberately. Jesus said, in effect: "Whosoever hears these sayings of mine and does them will be likened unto a man who is wise when he builds a house. He spends time and thought on the most important part of the building — *the foundation*. He makes sure the foundation is correct." So — the person who hears the Word of God and believes the Word of God is like a wise man who built his house upon a rock. The house was completed, the floods came, the winds blew, the storms beat upon the house — but it did not fall. . . "FOR IT WAS FOUNDED UPON A ROCK."

Please notice: The Lord Jesus did not mention the contractor, the carpenters, the masons — nor how efficiently they constructed the house. He did not say that the house stood because it was built in a unique way, nor because it had a well-constructed roof. It did not stand because of the braces in the walls. There is not one word said about the roof, the braces, nor is there one word said about whether the house was built of brick, wood, or stone. The reason the house did not fall is very clear: *It was founded upon a rock* — a solid *foundation*. The secret of the house weathering the storms and floods was the foundation.

In Bible study it is always helpful to find the first time a word, a doctrine, or a subject is mentioned. "Rock" is mentioned for the first time in Exodus 17:6: "Behold, I will stand before thee there upon the rock in Horeb; and thou shalt smite the rock, and there shall come water out of it, that the people may drink. And Moses did so in the sight of the elders of Israel."

Time and space will not permit me to go into detail concerning what preceded this unusual miracle — but briefly, the children of Israel were in the desert. They were thirsty, they were grumbling — and there was no water. When Moses sought the Lord, He assured Moses that He would go before him and stand upon the rock in Horeb. Moses was instructed to smite the rock, and water would come forth. Moses obeyed, God worked a miracle — and water gushed from the rock.

Jesus is *our Rock* — symbolized by the rock which Moses smote. When Moses struck the rock at Horeb, he was pointing to Calvary and the time when Jesus would be smitten. But note the *second* time Moses prayed about water, and God instructed him to produce water out of the rock:

Moses was at that time instructed to *speak* to the rock — but he did not obey. He *smote* the rock — and because he disobeyed God, he was not permitted to enter into the Promised Land. Moses committed the "sin unto death." It seems a small matter to strike a rock instead of speaking to it — but we must remember that the rock typifies Jesus — and Jesus could not be smitten but once for our sins. God instructed Moses to speak to the rock. To-day we are to preach the Word. We are to tell forth the Word, for "faith cometh by hearing, and hearing by the Word of God." Jesus was smitten once, for all, forever — never to be smitten again; and He is The Rock, the Chief Cornerstone. He is the Rock the builders pushed aside — but whom God has made the Chief Cornerstone.

In Daniel 2:45 we see the stone cut out of the mountain without hands — the stone which will eventually fill the whole earth. That stone (or rock) is none other than the Lord Jesus Christ. In Matthew 16:18 we hear Jesus announcing to the disciples, "...Upon this rock I will build my church; and the gates of hell shall not prevail against it." (The rock, of course, is Jesus). Peter had just confessed that Jesus was the Christ, the Son of God — and HE is the Rock upon which the church is built. Peter is *not* that rock, as some religions teach.

We read an interesting fact in Matthew 21:44 "And whosoever shall fall on this stone shall be broken: but on whomsoever it shall fall, it will grind him to powder." Just what is meant by the phrase, "Whosoever shall fall upon this stone shall be broken"? That means that if we literally fling ourselves upon Jesus, or cast ourselves upon Him in faith, we will be broken and made meet for the Master's use. We will be crushed and molded into a vessel of honor instead of dishonor; but if we do *not* fall upon the Stone, the Stone will fall upon us in judgment, grinding us into powder!

Christ the Stone is revealed in Scripture in three ways:

First — *to Israel* Christ the Stone is a stumbling stone . . . a rock of offense (Isa. 8:14-15; Rom. 9:32-33; I Cor. 1:23; I Peter 2:8). Israel was looking and longing for a royal monarch to present himself in splendor and power; but Jesus came as a lamb — meek, lowly, humble. Therefore, to Israel He was "a stumbling stone and a rock of offense."

In the second place, *to the church* Christ the Stone is the Foundation, the Chief Cornerstone, the Headstone (I Cor. 3:11; Eph. 2:20-22; I Peter 2:4-5). The church is built upon Jesus; He is the solid, sure foundation.

In the third place, to the *Gentile world powers* Jesus is the smiting stone of destruction and judgment (Dan. 2:34). One day the Stone "cut out of the mountain without hands" will grind the wicked into powder in fierce judgment. The nation of Israel *stumbled* over Jesus the Stone. The New Testament church is *built* upon Jesus the Stone. The Gentile world powers will be *broken* by the Stone when Jesus comes in judgment at the consummation of all things.

The first mention of a word is important in Scripture — but the last mention of that word is also important. The rock is mentioned for the last time in Revelation 6:15-16. Those who refuse to receive the Lord Jesus (the Rock of our salvation) will beg the *rocks* (plural) to fall upon them and hide them from the face of Him who sits on the throne. Jesus is The Rock — and Jesus will be sitting on the throne when kings, mighty men and great men will beg God to cover them with rocks. *Their prayer will be unanswered!*

It is interesting to note that the first temptation the devil hurled at Jesus (the Rock) was a challenge to change rocks into bread

(Matt. 4:3). When He was taken down from the cross, He was placed in a new tomb hewn out of stone — a giant rock.

Jesus is the Rock, the Chief Cornerstone, the sure Foundation. When we build upon Him our house will never fall. The tornadoes of hell may come, the hurricanes of the damned may beat upon us, the floods of wickedness may sweep all around us, but if we build upon Jesus, we will stand! "Verily, verily, I say unto you, He that HEARETH my word, and believeth on Him that sent me, hath everlasting life" (John 5:24). "But as many as received Him, to them gave He power to become the sons of God, even to them that believe on His name" (John 1:12). If we hear the Word, if we receive Jesus as the Word tells us to do, *we will be standing when the world is on fire!* "If God be for us, who can be against us?" (Romans 8:31).

Before we go further in this message, permit me to ask you, Are you building on *The Rock?* Are you making preparation for the eternity that lies ahead by building upon The Rock, Christ Jesus? If not, *begin today!*

ROCKS

"And everyone that heareth these sayings of mine, and doeth them not, shall be likened unto a foolish man, which built his house upon the sand" (Matt. 7:26). Jesus here declares that the person who hears the Word of God but does not obey what he hears, is like a man building a house on a beach or a sand dune.

The first mention of foolish people in the Bible is in Deuteronomy 32:1. In speaking to the children of Israel, Moses cried out: "Because I will publish the name of the Lord: ascribe ye greatness unto our God. HE IS THE ROCK, His work is perfect: for all His ways are judgment: a God of truth and without iniquity, just and right is He. They have corrupted themselves, their spot is not the spot of His children: they are a perverse and crooked generation. Do ye thus requite the Lord, O FOOLISH PEOPLE AND UNWISE? Is not He thy father that hath bought thee?

Hath He not made thee, and established thee?" Here Moses pro-claims to Israel that *God is their Rock,* and that they have cor-rupted themselves because they refused to hear the word of Jehovah God. They are "foolish and unwise."

Perhaps someone is asking, "Mr. Greene, *where are the rocks* mentioned in the title of the message?" Here is the answer: *What is sand?* Have you ever stopped to consider that sand is nothing more than soil that has had a good bath in the river or ocean? Suppose we let Webster tell us: "Sand is the fine debris of rocks." That means that sand is little rocks.

I was reared on the farm. Many times I have walked barefooted in the drain ditches around the field and wiggled my toes in the sand which had been produced by the rain washing away the soil, leaving the tiny little rocks. Every person who reads these lines at this moment is building on the solid Rock, Christ Jesus — or else he is building on r-o-c-k-s (sand).

Can you imagine an intelligent person pouring concrete or laying a brick foundation for a house on the beach or on a sand dune? It is true that houses are built along the beach — but the contractor first digs deep to get a solid footing, or else piling is driven deep into the ground, then the foundation is laid and the building is constructed. Only a fool would go out on the beach and begin building a house or laying bricks on the shifting sand.

Beloved, it is nothing short of pure foolishness to *hear* the Word of God and not obey it. Have you heard that the wages of sin is death? Have you heard that it is better to lose your hand, your foot, your eye, than to have these members and be cast into hell, into the fire that never shall be quenched? Have you heard, "Come unto me, and I will give you rest"? Have you read that whosoever shall call upon the name of the Lord shall be saved? Have you heard the solemn warning in the Bible concerning hell-fire and damnation? Have you heard the precious story of God's love and His gift of the Lord Jesus to hell-deserving sinners? If you have heard these warnings, if you have heard the invitation, and yet you pay no attention to either, you are playing the part of a fool. You are building on sand — little rocks — and when the winds begin to blow and the floods begin to come, the first storm will undermine your house and it will fall!

There may be many religions that are attractive to live by — but when the tornadoes of God's judgment strike, there is only one foundation that is sure to stand — and *that Foundation is Jesus.* If you are building on any religion except that of the Lord Jesus Christ (Christianity), you are building on sinking sand — little rocks. Are you building on The Rock? If you are, your house will never fall. Are you building on r-o-c-k-s? You may not realize it now, but your religion is *already* on the rocks if you are building on r-o-c-k-s. It cannot and will not stand in the hour of judgment.

RAGS

Rags are not a very inviting subject. I know of nothing more disgusting or less inviting than dirty, filthy, rotten rags. Yet — the Bible mentions rags in three different Scriptures.

In Proverbs 23:21 rags are mentioned in connection with the drunkard. Drink brings poverty and rags — not only to the drunkard, but to his *family* as well. You have witnessed this truth in your own community — or perhaps in your own home.

In Jeremiah 38:11-12 rags are used as pads under the arms of the prophet Jeremiah, when he was pulled up out of the pit into which he had been placed because of his fearless proclamation of the warnings of God concerning judgment.

Then, rags are mentioned by Isaiah — and this is the Scripture we will study in our present message: "But we are all as an unclean thing, and ALL OUR RIGHTEOUSNESSES ARE AS FILTHY RAGS..." (Isa. 64:6a). Now, what is the Holy Spirit saying to you and to me, through the writer Isaiah? Could God find no better word than *rags* to describe what He is saying to us? I think there is an unmistakable point here. Had God used some term pertaining to millionaires, the *poor man* might have missed the spiritual application; but I believe that both the rich AND the poor understand *rags.* Some rich men have never had an occasion to be closely associated with rags, but many men have become rich because they have taken from the poor, and they have witnessed rags as a result of their greed and selfishness. So — young and old, rich and poor, educated and uneducated — ALL know the meaning of rags and what they represent. Rags suggest poverty. Rags suggest uncleanness. Rags suggest rottenness.

What God is saying to you and me is simply this: It matters not how good we live, how clean we live, how honest we are, how upright we may be. It makes no difference how much we give — nor how much we sacrifice in giving. All the good things we can do throughout the days of our life — all, yes, ALL we *do, give,* or *live,* add up to nothing better than dirty, filthy, despicable, rotten rags — a horribly uninviting sight, to state it mildly.

God does not want filthy rags. He wants you and me to come to Him and present ourselves as unclean — totally depraved, rotten in sin, fit only for the spiritual garbage can. He wants us to bring our rags to Him and let Him exchange the white robe of heaven (the righteousness of Jesus Christ) for them. He (Jesus) who *knew* no sin, was made sin for us that we in Him might be made the righteousness of God (II Cor. 5:21). *Christ is our righteousness.* Christ is our covering — and though our sins be as scarlet, when we are wrapped in the robe of His righteousness we are as white as the driven snow!

"Not by works of righteousness which we have done, but according to His mercy He saved us, by the washing of regeneration, and renewing of the Holy Ghost" (Titus 3:5).

"For by grace are ye saved through faith; and that not of yourselves: it is the gift of God: not of works, lest any man should boast" (Eph. 2:8-9).

Dear reader, are you wearing *rags* — or are you wearing Heaven's best robe? Time and space will not permit me to quote here the parable of the prodigal son, but you can read the story in

Luke 15. When the prodigal son left his father's house, he had money. He took his inheritance with him. He was clothed in garments that were respectable and clean. But he sowed to the flesh — and he woke up feeding swine! His clothes were in tatters, he was barefooted, he had the filth and stench of the hog pen upon his person and upon the rags he wore.

Sitting beside the hog pen, watching the pigs gobble up the husks, the prodigal "came to himself" and said, "My father has servants who have bread and to spare — while I perish with hunger! I will arise and go to my father, and I will tell him that I have sinned against Heaven, that I have grievously sinned in his sight, and am not worthy to be called his son. . . . I just want to be a servant!"

That was the little speech the prodigal gave to himself as he sat by the hog pen. . . . Thank God he did not change his story. He did arise, he did go to his father. When the father ran and fell on his neck and kissed him, it did not change the prodigal's feelings about himself. He confessed his sins — and the father said, "BRING FORTH THE BEST ROBE AND PUT IT ON HIM!" He put the best shoes on his feet and filled the banquet table with the best of food. God gives only Heaven's best to those of us who will bring our rags to Him. Bring your rags to Jesus, sinner. He will wrap you in a robe of righteousness — *the best robe Heaven has!*

LEAVES

We have discussed rocks, we have taken a look at rags — and now let us consider *leaves*.

Unlike rags, leaves are very beautiful. I know of nothing more beautiful than the mountains in the fall, when at the first frost, Mother Nature with one giant stroke of her brush, paints the hillsides with every color of the rainbow! There is such beauty as no artist could ever produce, though he be a master of the art.

There is no season I love better than the spring, when the

green leaves begin to appear. The cold winter blast is over, the snow and ice are gone. Mother Earth sends the warm sap through the trunks of the trees, and new growth appears, painting the hillsides in one of nature's most pleasant colors — *green*.

The first mention of leaves is in the first book of the Bible and has to do with the first family, Adam and Eve. You know the story. God created man — and then gave him Eve to be his help-mate. He placed them in the most beautiful garden ever known, where there was every tree that was beautiful, and every tree that produced fruit good to eat. God visited the garden daily in the cool of the day — but Satan in his envy and jealousy would not permit this marvelous home to continue for very long.

One day Satan stepped into the garden and asked Eve a question. In the course of the conversation, Eve yielded to the temptation he presented, and ate the fruit of the one tree God had forbidden to them. (Adam was clearly instructed that the day he ate of that fruit, he would die.) Eve ate, she gave to her husband Adam, and HE *ate*. They died spiritually, their eyes were opened, and they saw the most disgusting, sickening, heart-breaking sight imaginable. They saw their nakedness!

They were horrified. They immediately began working to correct their sad plight. They did not run to seek help from their Maker, they did not cry to God for mercy. They now had wisdom, they now had knowledge . . . they could correct their mistake (so they thought). They sewed fig leaves together and made aprons. They put the aprons on their naked bodies. I am sure that to their *own* satisfaction, the shame of their nakedness did not appear. Everything was lovely until . . . yes, *until they heard the voice of God,* walking in the garden in the cool of the day! They heard the voice of their Creator, their Friend, their daily Visitor — the One with whom they had had perfect fellowship until now.

When they heard His voice, they ran and hid themselves among the trees. God cried out, "Adam — where art thou?" and

Adam answered with this sad testimony: "Lord, . . . *I'm hiding among the trees.* I heard your voice — and I was afraid . . . for I am naked!" When God asked Adam who told him he was naked, Adam placed the blame on Eve. Eve placed the blame on the serpent. But neither their excuses nor their hiding did them any good. God found their hiding place; He paid no attention to their excuses. He condemned their figleaf garments and provided coats of skins — at the expense of the blood of innocent animals.

From that moment until now, God has demanded a blood sacrifice for the remission of sins. In spite of the teaching of all the liberals and modernists in the world, *without the shedding of blood, there is no remission!* (Heb. 9:22). Regardless of what any man preaches or teaches, regardless of what any author writes, the choice is still *blood* or *hell.* God will not accept any sacrifice that is not provided at the price of blood.

Jesus shed His blood on the cross. The Lamb of God was slain, that we might have remission of sins. The blood of Jesus Christ, God's Son, cleanses us from all sin (I John 1:7). We are not redeemed with anything that will corrupt. We are redeemed with the precious blood of the Lamb! (I Peter 1:18-21).

Your religion may be beautiful to live by — it may be attractive, it may be inviting; but if your religion is produced through the wisdom of man and by the labors of man's hands, that religion is just as empty and profitless as *leaves.* I warn you that "religious leaves" can never correct the shame of your sin before the eyes of God. It may satisfy you, but *it will not satisfy Him.*

There are many religions that are attractive to *live* by, but there is only one religion that will do to *die* by — and that is the religion of the Lord Jesus Christ: *Christianity,* salvation by faith in His finished work. He died on a tree . . . a tree that had no leaves to shade His aching brow. It was a cross — a *bloody* cross. Unless you are covered by *His blood,* your religion is a religion of leaves.

Matthew 21:18-20 tells us of one day when Jesus was returning to the city of Jerusalem, and He was hungry: "Now in the morning as he returned into the city, he hungered. And when he saw a fig tree in the way, he came to it, and found nothing thereon, but leaves only, and said unto it, Let no fruit grow on thee henceforward for ever. And presently the fig tree withered away. And when the disciples saw it, they marvelled, saying, How soon is the fig tree withered away!"

Whether it be a nation such as Israel, or a church, a minister, or a layman, the Lord Jesus is looking for *fruit* — not leaves. Leaves are beautiful to look upon. They serve to shade us from the hot summer sun — but they are of no value. If the owner of an orchard should gather all of the leaves from all of his trees, he could not sell them for enough money to pay a laborer to gather them.

I live in the peach-growing section of South Carolina. There are millions of peach trees in this state. Sometimes a late frost kills the blooms, and the fruit does not mature — but the leaves grow even larger and more luxurious when there is no fruit than they do when the trees are hanging with delicious peaches. The leaves absorb all of the food for growth that the peaches would have used had they developed. When there are no peaches, there is an abundant crop of leaves — but not one orchard owner bothers to gather them! Fruit is what he desires — and in the spiritual aspect, *Jesus* is looking for fruit. When He came to the fig tree, and there were no figs, He cursed it. It withered and died.

Jesus said, "I am the true vine, and my Father is the husband-man. Every branch in me that beareth not fruit he taketh away: and every branch that beareth fruit, he purgeth it, that it may bring forth *more* fruit. Now ye are clean through the Word which I have spoken unto you. Abide in me, and I in you. As the branch cannot bear fruit of itself, except it abide in the vine; no more can ye, except ye abide in me. I am the vine, ye are the branches: He that abideth in me, and I in him, the same bringeth forth much fruit: for without me ye can do nothing. If a man abide not in me, he is cast forth as a branch, and is withered; and men gather them and cast them into the fire, and they are burned. If ye abide in me, and my words abide in you, ye shall ask what ye will, and it shall be done unto you. Herein is my Father glorified, *that ye bear much fruit; so shall ye be my disciples*" (John 15:1-8).

All born-again believers bear some fruit. Jesus said some bear thirty, some sixty, and some an hundredfold; but there is no such thing as a born-again child of God who is entirely fruitless. Life produces some kind of fruit. It may not be in abundance, but if we are born-again, *we will* produce fruit. Jesus wants us to glorify Him by bearing "MUCH fruit."

Notice in the Scripture we have just read, the fruit-bearer is purged — and brings forth *"more* fruit." But there are those who bring forth *much fruit,* and these are the children who glorify the Father. He is glorified in us and by us when we bear much fruit. What counts with God is not the outward show, nor the size of the ministry — but the fruit produced as a *result* of the service — FRUIT, not leaves. Jesus is looking for Christian workers — men and women, young men and young women, boys and girls — who will bear *much* fruit.

In closing, let me ask you, dear reader: "Are you on *The Rock,* Christ Jesus? Are you building on the solid Rock, the Chief Cornerstone — or are you building on the r-o-c-k-s . . . sinking sand?" If you are building on THE Rock, you will stand in the hour of judgment; but if you are building on the little rocks, on the sand, your building will crumble. It has no foundation, it cannot stand.

Are you trusting in your good works — in how you live, what you give, the things you do — to get you inside Heaven's door? If you are, just remember that *all of our righteousnesses are as filthy rags.* We cannot do enough, we cannot give enough, we cannot live good enough, to enter Heaven. We must be clothed with the garments of God's righteousness — *the blood of Jesus Christ.* HE is our righteousness. So if you are trying to merit Heaven by good works or by a good life, remember that all the good you can do will add up to no more than filthy rags!

Adam and Eve attempted to correct this mistake by the labor of their own hands — but they failed. Are you trying to cover up your sin by the good things you do with your hands? Are you trying to cover up your sin by being a good church member? The hiding place of Adam and Eve was no good. Their excuses failed. The judgment of Almighty God fell upon them! Fig leaves would not cover sin — only blood could do that. And remember that excuses and spiritual fig leaves will not cover *your* sin today. Nothing will do that except the blood of Jesus. If you are not a believer, bow your head and trust Jesus NOW.

Dear Christian, remember Jesus wants fruit — *more* fruit, *much* fruit — not leaves. If you are a believer and you are not fully consecrated, surrender soul, spirit, and body to Jesus this moment, to His name's honor and glory. May God help you and me to check our lives, and see if we are bearing fruit to the glory of God.

Who—What—Why?

Chapter II

Who — What — Why?

"And when he was gone forth into the way, there came one running, and kneeled to him, and asked him, Good Master, what shall I do that I may inherit eternal life? And Jesus said unto him, Why callest thou me good? There is none good but one, that is, God. Thou knowest the commandments, Do not commit adultery, Do not kill, Do not steal, Do not bear false witness, Defraud not, Honor thy father and mother.

"And he answered and said unto Him, Master, all these have I observed from my youth. Then Jesus beholding him loved him, and said unto him, One thing thou lackest: go thy way, sell whatsoever thou hast, and give to the poor, and thou shalt have treasure in heaven: and come, take up the cross, and follow me. And he was sad at that saying, and went away grieved: for he had great possessions.

"And Jesus looked round about, and saith unto his disciples, How hardly shall they that have riches enter into the kingdom of God! And the disciples were astonished at his words. But Jesus answereth again, and saith unto them, Children, how hard it is for them that trust in riches to enter into the kingdom of God! It is easier for a camel to go through the eye of a needle, than for a rich man to enter into the kingdom of God.

"And they were astonished out of measure, saying among themselves, *Who then can be saved?* And Jesus looking upon them saith, With men it is impossible, but not with God: for *with God all things are possible*" (Mark 10:17-27).

27

The disciples were amazed when Jesus said "How hardly shall they that have riches enter into the kingdom of God! It is easier for a camel to go through the eye of a needle than for a rich man to enter the kingdom of God!" These clearly understandable words caused bewilderment among the disciples, and they questioned among themselves, saying, "WHO THEN CAN BE SAVED?"

Jesus knew their thoughts just as He knows the thoughts and intent of the hearts of all men. He looked upon His disciples and said, "With men it is impossible, but not with God: for WITH GOD ALL THINGS ARE POSSIBLE!"

The disciples asked a good question: *"Who,* then, can be saved?" We need to know the answer because there are varied and sundry ideas as to who CAN become a Christian. There are many doctrines in the land concerning the elect, the predestined. Who *can,* and who can*not,* be saved? If we want the Bible answer, we must go to the Bible — not to books of doctrine, catechism, or rules of religion.

I love Paul's text: "Let God be true, and every man a liar" (Rom. 3:4). When I study the Word of God, I believe what the Word declares and mark off what other men say. We need what the Bible teaches concerning "Who can be saved?"

There is a sect known as "Jehovah's Witnesses" who say they are the 144,000. They claim to be the elect, and declare that they are the ones who will be saved in the end. Another group, the hyper-Calvinists, teaches that those who are elected will be saved, and those not elected cannot be saved. Many Roman Catholics teach that the church of Rome is THE Church, and that all are lost who are outside of that church. There are other groups too numerous to mention — but I repeat, "Let God be true, and every man a liar."

The answer to the question, "Who then can be saved?" is found in the words of Jesus: "For God so loved the world, that he gave his only begotten Son, that *whosoever believeth in him* should not perish, but have everlasting life" (John 3:16).

God Almighty loved the whole world so deeply, He gave His only begotten Son, that *whosoever will believe on Him* shall not perish, but have everlasting life. *"Whosoever believeth?"* That verse means exactly what it says. The white man, the black man, the red man, the yellow man, the pauper, the millionaire, the educated, the ignorant, the down-and-out, the up-and-out — *whosoever believes.* If you are in the world, you are one of those for whom God gave His dear Son. You are one of those for whom Jesus died.

Peter says "Amen" to John 3:16 in these words: "The Lord is not slack concerning his promise, as some men count slackness: but is longsuffering to us-ward, not willing that any should perish, but that all should come to repentance" (II Peter 3:9).

According to these words, inspired of the Holy Ghost, it is not God's will that one single soul should perish, but that every individual should be saved. That does not mean that every individual WILL be saved, but every person who drops into hell will do so because he refused to trust Jesus.

"My little children, these things write I unto you, that ye sin not. And if any man sin, we have an Advocate with the Father, Jesus Christ the righteous: And he is the propitiation for our sins: and not for ours only, but also for the sins of the whole world" (I John 2:1-2).

Jesus paid the price for every sin that has ever been committed, or ever will be committed, when He willingly shed His blood on the cross. Just before His head came to rest on His pulseless breast, He said, "It is *finished!*" He completed the plan of salvation and paid the ransom in full — yea, for the sins of the whole wide world. He purchased redemption for *every* sinner.

Jesus came into the world on a singular mission. Trainloads of books have been written about Him, but Luke sums up that mission in just a few words: *"For the Son of man is come to seek*

and to save that which was lost" (Luke 19:10). The Holy Spirit
tells us that Jesus came to seek out and save *lost people*. If you
will realize you are lost, *you can be saved.*

Paul tells us that Jesus is able to save "to the uttermost" all
who will come unto God by Him (Heb. 7:25). According to this
Scripture, Jesus came to save — "even to the uttermost!" — ALL
who will come to God by Him.

In Isaiah 53:6 we read an enlightening declaration: "ALL we
like sheep have gone astray; we have turned every one to his
own way; and the Lord [Jehovah God] hath laid on him [Jesus]
the iniquity of us all." (Please notice that this verse begins and
ends with the word *"all."*) *All* we like sheep have gone astray...
ALL have sinned and come short of the glory of God. There is
none righteous, no, not one; but God the Father laid on Jesus,
the Lamb, the only begotten Son, the sins of US ALL.

Those who believe and teach that some are elected to be saved
while others are not elected, should use the text Jesus used in
speaking to Israel, God's chosen nation: "Search the Scriptures;
for in them ye think ye have eternal life: and they are they
which testify of me. And *ye will not come to me,* that ye might
have life" (John 5:39-40).

Why were these people lost? Why were they eternally doomed?
Was it because they were not elected? Was it because they were
not predestined? Were they not among the chosen? Jesus clearly
said, "And YE WILL NOT come to me, that ye might have
life." According to those words, all who drop into the pits of the
damned will do so because they *refused to come to Jesus* that
they might have life. God never created one soul for hell, nor
did He create hell for one soul. Matthew 25:41 clearly teaches
us that hell was prepared for the devil and his angels.

Genesis 1:1: "In the beginning God created the heaven and
the earth." There is no mention nor suggestion that God created
hell when He created the heaven and the earth. God had no
need for hell. In the beginning there was no devil and there

were no sinners. Hell was prepared at a later date and it was not prepared for man.

Heaven is prepared for those who choose to serve Jesus. "In my Father's house are many mansions. I go to prepare a place for YOU," Jesus said in John 14:1. But only people who prepare for Heaven can enter there. Heaven is a *prepared place* for a *prepared people*. All who will come to Jesus and trust Him as their Saviour can *enter* Heaven. There is a home reserved for all who will trust Jesus and receive Him as their personal Saviour.

"Blessed be the God and Father of our Lord Jesus Christ, which according to his abundant mercy hath begotten us again unto a lively hope by the resurrection of Jesus Christ from the dead, to an inheritance incorruptible, and undefiled, and that fadeth not away, reserved in Heaven for you, who are kept by the power of God through faith unto salvation ready to be revealed in the last time" (I Peter 1:3-5).

Do you have salvation? If you do not, it is not God's fault — it is your fault. Jesus paid the sin-debt, He paid the ransom note, He purchased salvation. "Whosoever will, let him come.... Whosoever shall call upon the name of the Lord shall be saved.... They that come unto me, I will in no wise cast out." If you are not saved it is not God's fault — it is your own. You will not come to Jesus that you might have life.

WHAT

What IS salvation? If we listen to men, we will hear various answers to that question. But we will turn to the Word of God — the textbook for the Christian.

In Acts 2:47 we read, "And the Lord added to the church daily such as were [being] saved." The words "saved," "salvation," and "new birth" have been outlawed from many pulpits today. All some dear people ever hear is, "Would you like to unite with us? Would you like to join our church?" Or perhaps

"Would you like to follow Christ in baptism?" It is entirely possible to join a church, be baptized, unite with the greatest assembly on earth — and still not possess salvation.

"Salvation is of the Lord" (Ps. 3:8; Jonah 2:9). Salvation is not *something;* salvation is someONE. Salvation is life: "And you hath he quickened [made alive] who were dead in trespasses and sins." All sinners are spiritually dead. When the sinner is saved, life comes in — "Christ in you, the hope of glory" (Col. 1:27). "There is therefore now no condemnation to them which are in Christ Jesus" (Rom. 8:1).

Salvation is a *birth.* The longer I study the Bible and the more I try to preach the Word of God, the more I enjoy the sermons of Jesus. Why does the Holy Spirit use the term "birth" in connection with salvation? In the grand and glorious first chapter of John, we read, "He came unto his own, and his own received Him not. But as many as received him, to them gave he power to become the sons of God, even to them that believe on his name: *Which were born...born of God!"* (John 1:11-13).

John's Gospel is the "Salvation Gospel" (John 20:30-31). It opens with the declaration that salvation is a birth, and God is the author of that birth. God gives the power of birth when we, by faith, receive the Lord Jesus.

Nicodemus was one of the first converts of Jesus. We find the account in John, Chapter three. Nicodemus was a ruler of the Jews — an outstanding religionist with a Master's degree. He came to Jesus by night, and opened the conversation by saying, "Rabbi, we know that thou art a teacher come from God: for no man can do these miracles that thou doest, except God be with him." I do not know what answer Nicodemus expected from Jesus, but the answer he received was pure gospel: "Verily, verily, I say unto thee, Except a man be born again, he cannot see the kingdom of God." Nicodemus was a sincere seeker of truth, and he, therefore, asked, "How can a man be born when he is old?"

Nicodemus was thinking in terms of the natural; but before we can possess salvation, we must accept the *supernatural*. The natural man is lost, at enmity with God — and he cannot save *himself*. Salvation is from without and from above. Salvation comes INTO the heart of the sinner when he accepts the miracle of God's grace.

Nicodemus wanted to know how a man could be born when he is old. Jesus replied, "Except a man be born of water [the Word] [John 15:3; Eph. 5:26; I Peter 1:23; Rom. 10:17] and of the Spirit, he cannot enter into the kingdom of God. That which is born of the flesh is flesh; that which is born of the Spirit is spirit. Marvel not that I said unto thee, Ye must be born again" (John 3:1-7).

Notice the number of times the word "born" is used in these verses. When we think of birth, we think of life. We think of a new-born babe, a new personality, and that is exactly what happens when we are saved. To be saved is to become a new creation: "Therefore if any man be in Christ, he is a new creature: old things are passed away; behold, all things are become new" (II Cor. 5:17).

Salvation is not uniting or joining — but *being born from above*. The new birth is God's miracle when we accept the Word — the Seed that produces life (I Peter 1:23, John 5:24). Salvation is becoming partaker of divine nature. "Whereby are given unto us exceeding great and precious promises *that by these* YE MIGHT BE MADE PARTAKERS OF DIVINE NATURE, having escaped the corruption that is in the world through lust" (II Peter 1:4).

A Christian actually possesses divine nature. The divine nature that abides within every believer is the Holy Ghost:

"If any man have not the Spirit of Christ, he is none of his" (Rom. 8:9).

"The Spirit itself beareth witness with our spirit that we are the children of God" (Rom. 8:16).

"As many as are led by the Spirit of God, they are the sons of God" (Rom. 8:14).

"Grieve not the Holy Spirit of God whereby ye are sealed unto the day of redemption" (Eph. 4:30).

"Christ in you, the hope of glory" (Col. 1:27).

These verses clearly teach that a believer is a possessor of divine nature. Salvation is eternal life abiding in the bosom of the believer. Salvation is being transplanted out of a kingdom of darkness into THE Kingdom of Light.

"Giving thanks unto the Father, which hath made us meet to be partakers of the inheritance of the saints in light: Who hath delivered us from the power of darkness, and hath translated us into the kingdom of his dear Son: In whom we have redemption through his blood, even the forgiveness of sins" (Col. 1:12-14).

Jesus said, "I am the Light of the World." Therefore, His kingdom is the kingdom of light. When we believe on the Lord Jesus Christ we are taken out of the kingdom of darkness and placed over in the kingdom of light.

"But ye, brethren, are not in darkness, that that day should overtake you as a thief. Ye are all the children of light, and the children of the day: we are not of the night, nor of darkness" (I Thess. 5:4-5).

It is impossible to be a born again child of God and not know it. If it is possible for a new baby to be born into a home without anyone knowing it — if it is possible for a person to be raised from the dead without knowing it — if it is possible for one to step from a dark room into a lighted room without knowing it, then it is possible to be saved and *not* know it.

Salvation is a birth.

Salvation is a resurrection from the dead.

Salvation is becoming a new creation, possessing divine nature.

Salvation is Christ in you.

Salvation is passing from a kingdom of darkness into The Kingdom of Light.

Salvation is far more than church membership, confirmation, baptism, living a good life or doing "the best you can."

"And the Lord added unto the church daily such as were [being] saved."

WHY?

We have considered who can be saved — and according to the Word of God we find that "whosoever will" may come.

We have considered the "WHAT" of salvation — and discovered that it is God's miracle, not man's ability or righteousness.

Now — *WHY does God save the sinner?*

It was God who "so loved the world." It was God who gave His only begotten Son. It was God the Father who turned His head while Jesus cried out, "My God! My God! Why hast thou forsaken me?" It was God who smote the Lamb whose blood purchased redemption, paid the ransom note, and made it possible for sinners to be saved.

But WHY does God save the sinner? Is God in the fire insurance business? Ask most church members why a sinner should be saved, and they will immediately reply, "In order to miss hell." Ask the average church member why God saves the sinner, and he will answer, "To keep that sinner from burning in hell." Is that the reason God saves us? Are we worthy of salvation? Does God save us just so we will not burn in the pits of the damned? The only place to find the answer is in the Word of God:

"How shall we escape, if we neglect so great salvation; which at the first began to be spoken by the Lord, and was confirmed unto us by them that heard him. . . . But we see Jesus, who was made a little lower than the angels for the suffering of death, crowned with glory and honor; that he *by the grace of God* should taste death for every man. . . . Forasmuch then as the children are partakers of flesh and blood, he also himself likewise took part of the same; that through death he might destroy him that had the power of death, that is, the devil; And deliver them, who through fear of death were all their lifetime subject to bondage" (Heb. 2:3, 9, 14, 15).

"BY THE GRACE OF GOD," Jesus took a body, came into this world willingly, was tempted in all points as we are, yet was without sin. He willingly lived here for more than thirty-three years, willingly laid His life down in order that He might taste death for every man, destroy "him that had the power of death" (the devil), and deliver men from the fear of death. All this Jesus did "by the grace of God."

Centuries before the birth of Christ, the Psalmist wrote, "Nevertheless, *he saved them for his name's sake,* that he might make his mighty power to be known" (Ps. 106:8).

Paul clearly tells us why God saves sinners: "And grieve not the Holy Spirit of God, whereby ye are sealed unto the day of redemption. Let all bitterness, and wrath, and anger, and clamor, and evil speaking, be put away from you, with all malice: And be ye kind one to another, tender-hearted, forgiving one another, even as God FOR CHRIST'S SAKE hath forgiven you" (Eph. 4:30-32).

Why does God save the sinner? Why does God give us salvation by grace through faith? "FOR CHRIST'S SAKE!"

But why does God save us for Christ's sake? The Word of God answers:

"And you hath he quickened, who were dead in trespasses and sins: Wherein in time past ye walked according to the course of this world, according to the prince of the power of the air, the spirit that now worketh in the children of disobedience: Among whom also we all had our conversation in times past in the lusts of our flesh, fulfilling the desires of the flesh and of the mind; and were by nature the children of wrath, even as others. BUT GOD, who is rich in mercy, for HIS GREAT LOVE wherewith He loved us, Even when we were dead in sins, hath quickened us together with Christ, (by grace ye are saved;) AND HATH RAISED US UP TOGETHER AND MADE US SIT TOGETHER IN HEAVENLY PLACES IN CHRIST JESUS: THAT IN THE AGES TO COME HE MIGHT SHEW THE EXCEEDING RICHES OF HIS GRACE, IN HIS KINDNESS TOWARD US, THROUGH CHRIST JESUS. For by grace are ye saved through faith; and that not of yourselves: *it is the gift of God:* Not of works, lest any man should boast. For we are his workmanship, created in Christ Jesus unto good works, which God hath before ordained that we should walk in them" (Eph. 2:1-10).

God, *for Christ's sake,* has saved us — that in the ages to come He (God) may demonstrate "the exceeding riches of his grace" in the church, which will be displayed in the heavenlies when all things have been created new. We will have a new heaven, a new earth, and in the Pearly White City the Bride of God's beloved Son will be displayed. All creation in heaven and in earth will gaze upon the church "without spot or wrinkle or any such thing," after the church has been presented to Christ who purchased us with His own blood (Acts 20:28).

In Revelation 21, John saw seven new things: He saw a new heaven, a new earth, new peoples, the Lamb's wife (the New Jerusalem), the new temple, the new light, and the new Paradise with its river of the water of life.

"And there came unto me one of the seven angels which had the seven vials full of the seven last plagues, and talked with me, saying, Come hither, I will show thee the bride, the Lamb's wife. And he carried me away in the spirit to a great and high mountain, and showed me that great city the holy Jerusalem, descending out of heaven from God, having the glory of God: and her light was like unto a stone most precious, even like a jasper stone, clear as crystal" (Rev. 21:9-11).

In the verses that follow, John describes the city — the walls, the gates — the street; and then he says, "And I saw no temple therein: for the Lord God Almighty and the Lamb are the temple of it." The city needed neither sun nor moon, because the glory of God "did lighten it, and the Lamb is the light thereof. And the nations of them which are saved shall walk in the light of it: and the kings of the earth do bring their glory and honor into it."

The gates of that city will never be shut, and there shall be no night there. The kings and the nations will bring their glory and honor into it. To me, these facts teach that the Pearly White City which John saw descending from God out of Heaven is the place Jesus was speaking of when He said, "I go to prepare a place for you, and if I go I will come again, that where I am, there ye may be also." For more than nineteen hundred years, Jesus has been preparing that city.

John saw the city descend "from God out of heaven," but he did not see it come to rest upon the new earth. The city will be fifteen hundred miles wide, fifteen hundred miles long, and fifteen hundred miles high — it is foursquare. I believe it will be suspended between heaven and earth. The Scriptures tell us the nations "will walk in the light of it." The home of the church (the Pearly White City) will be displayed in the heavenlies just above the new earth, while all the nations (Israel and the nations who befriend her during the Tribulation, and the nations saved out of the Great Tribulation) will abide here on the new earth. They will walk in the light of that city, and will gaze upon the beauty and brightness of the home of the Lamb and the Lamb's wife — the church. God will display the exceeding riches of His grace in the church in the Pearly White City, suspended between heaven and earth.

The church is the pearl of great price . . . the prize possession of God the Father, God the Son, and God the Holy Ghost — and will be displayed throughout eternity in the Pearly White City. *God saves us for Christ's sake. God saves us in order to display the exceeding riches of His saving Grace* in us who make up the New Testament church.

"Husbands, love your wives, even as Christ also LOVED THE CHURCH, AND GAVE HIMSELF FOR IT; that he might sanctify and cleanse it with the washing of water by the word, THAT HE MIGHT PRESENT IT TO HIMSELF A GLORIOUS CHURCH, NOT HAVING SPOT, OR WRINKLE, OR ANY SUCH THING; but that it should be holy and without blemish" (Eph. 5:25-27).

We see clearly from the Word of God that His great love was extended to hell-deserving sinners in the Lord Jesus Christ. God permitted Jesus to die on the cross that we might be saved *for Christ's sake,* that we might become members of the body that is the Bride of the beloved Son. God saves us — not for our sakes, and not for the sake of keeping us out of hell — but for Christ's sake. We are saved entirely on the merit of His shed blood, His saving grace, the redemption HE bought. Christ, the only begotten Son of God, was made sin for us, that we in Jesus might become the righteousness of God in the New Testament church — without spot, without wrinkle — holy and without blemish.

Are YOU Saved? Do you possess eternal life? I did not ask you if you are a church member, or if you have a religion. (There are many religions, but there is only one salvation.) Jesus said, "I am the Way, the Truth, and the Life. No man cometh unto the Father but by me."

If you are not saved, *God loves you, Christ died for you* — and the *Holy Spirit* is calling you through this message. Give your heart to Jesus.

Who can be saved? YOU can! "Whosoever shall call upon the name of the Lord shall be saved" (Acts 2:21).

What IS salvation? Salvation is a birth — but God works the miracle of that birth. "As many as received Him, to them gave He power to become the sons of God, even to them that believe on His name, which were born. . . . born of God" (John 1:12-13).

God furnishes the power of birth, God performs the miracle of birth, when we receive the Lord Jesus.

Why does God want to save sinners? *"For Christ's sake,"* that in the ages to come, God in us (the New Testament church) on display in the Pearly White City might show the exceeding riches of His grace.

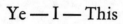
Ye — I — This

Chapter III

Ye — I — This

"And when Jesus departed thence, two blind men followed him, crying, and saying, Thou Son of David, have mercy on us. And when he was come into the house, the blind men came to him: and Jesus saith unto them, BELIEVE YE THAT I AM ABLE TO DO THIS? They said unto him, YEA LORD. Then touched he their eyes, saying, *According to your faith be it unto you.* And their eyes were opened . . ." (Matthew 9:27-30).

In these verses we have a beautiful picture of salvation, as well as divine healing. If there is any healing, it is divine . . . no man can heal. God has given us doctors and nurses; but if these bodies are healed, God must do the healing. In every case of healing recorded in the New Testament, there is always a lesson that goes deeper than *physical* healing. In every case where Jesus performed a miracle of healing, salvation always followed.

There are three aspects to be considered in each of these miracles:

1 — "Ye"
2 — "I"
3 — "This"

First — *our faith*. Without faith it is impossible to please God (Heb. 11:6).

Second — *His power*. "I am not ashamed of the gospel of Christ, for it is the power of God unto salvation" (Rom. 1:16). "As many as received him, to them gave he power to become the sons of God" (John 1:12).

Third — *our need*. Before God will supply the need of any person, that person must *confess* his need to God. The hardest thing I have to do as a minister is to convince sinners through the gospel that they need a Saviour. When a minister can make the unbeliever see that he needs a Saviour, the victory is nine-tenths won. We must make people see themselves as lost before we can get them saved.

This is the age when modernism and liberalism preach "the fatherhood of God and the brotherhood of man." The general idea is that no one is bad, everyone is good, and that a change of environment is all that is needed. But that is not true. The gospel fact is: *everybody* is bad; "there is *none* righteous — no, not *one*." We have gone astray and everyone needs a Saviour!

In our Scripture text, Jesus had just left the home of Jairus, where he had raised that nobleman's daughter. When He left the house, two blind men followed Him. No doubt they had heard much about Jesus and His miracles. They had a need — therefore, when He departed from Jairus' house they followed Him, and cried out, "Thou son of David, have mercy on us!"

They were making their request in the right attitude and in the right way. They recognized their need for mercy, they made no excuses; they knew they were blind, they did not blame any-one. They simply cried out for mercy. Following Jesus "until He was come into the house," the blind men came into the house with Him — they were not timid or backward, they did not stop outside. They knew their need, they wanted help. They had a deep desire to receive the blessing they felt in their hearts Jesus was able to give.

When they were in the house, Jesus spoke to them. So far as the record reveals, it is the first time He had uttered a word since they had been following Him. When He spoke, He simply asked, "Believe ye that I am able to do this?"

"YE"

God deals with individuals and His sense of value is far beyond man's imagination. Hear the Lord Jesus as He asks the solemn question, "What shall it profit a man, if he shall gain the whole world, and lose his own soul? or what shall a man give in exchange for his soul?" (Matt. 16:26).

Who would think of comparing one poor gutter-drunk with all the wealth of all the world! No one but Jesus! The soul (the inner man) of the vilest person on this earth is worth more than all the wealth of all the world — and I would not know how to express such worth if I knew what the figure would be. Salvation is an individual matter with Jesus. All through His public ministry He dealt with individuals ... blind Bartimaeus, Nicodemus, the woman at the well, Zacchaeus and many others In dealing with the blind men in our Scriptures, Jesus singled out the individual: "Believe YE? Do YOU believe that I am able to do what you are asking me to do?" That is the first step toward knowing Jesus. *If* we believe Jesus died and rose again; *if* we believe the blood of Jesus Christ, God's Son, cleanses us from all sin; *if* we believe that we are saved by grace through faith, "and that not of ourselves; it is the gift of God," we are ready for God's work in our heart. More than one hundred times in the Gospel of John we find the words "believe," "belief," or "receive" as having to do with salvation.

There is only one way to receive the miracle of God's grace: "As many as received HIM, to them gave he power to become the sons of God, even to them that believe on his name, which were born ... born of God" (John 1:12-13).

Paul tells us, "If our gospel be hid, it is hid to them that are lost: In whom the god of this world hath blinded the minds of them which believe not, lest the light of the glorious gospel of Christ, who is the image of God, should shine unto them" (II Cor. 4:3-4).

All sinners are blind, spiritually speaking. Their perception is darkened by sin. The sinner can never see nor understand the Way of Life, nor can he ever know or understand the peace of God, until the Lord Jesus opens his blinded mind. Jesus is the only One who can remove the scales from the minds of sinners and allow them, with the eye of faith, to see the gift of God — the finished work of the Lord Jesus when He purchased salvation at the tremendous price of His blood on the cross.

Salvation is an individual matter. The goodness of your mother and father will not save YOU. Certainly it is marvelous to be brought up in a Christian home. The environment of a Christian home has much to do with preparing children for the day when they themselves trust Jesus; but a Christian mother and father cannot save the child. No one can enter heaven on the salvation of the parent. We must be saved individually. Through one man, sin moved upon *all* men. Through the second Adam (the Lord Jesus) *redemption* has been purchased for all men. Each individual must be saved *as an individual*. God does not save collectively.

It is true we have the promise that if we believe, trust, and pray, we will see our loved ones saved. To the Philippian jailer Paul said, "Believe on the Lord Jesus Christ, and thou shalt be saved, and thy house" (Acts 16:31); but please notice that Paul and Silas *preached the Word* to all who were in that house, and *all* who were in the house were saved individually by trusting in Jesus. Yes, I believe in household salvation if the mother and father are born again, if they live right, pray right, and rear the children in the nurture and admonition of the Lord. "If ye abide in me, and my words abide in you, ye shall ask what ye will, and it shall be done unto you" (John 15:7). But we must keep in mind that the righteousness of one person cannot stand for (nor in the place of) the unrighteousness of another. We must be saved as an individual. "YE must be born again!" (John 3:3, 5, 7). When Jesus spoke His first words to the two blind men, He asked, "Believe YE?"

"I AM ABLE"

Jesus was able to do what the blind men asked. He could have spoken a word and the blind eyes would have opened instantaneously. But that is not God's way of dealing with men. We must first believe that He has the power to do what we ask, and when we believe that He has the power, He will *demonstrate* that power, supplying our every need. To the blind men Jesus said, "YE have the *need;* I have the *power.* But do YE BELIEVE that I have the power and the ability to open your blinded eyes?"

The blind men did not ask to put their hands on Jesus; they did not ask Him to come a little closer to them. They did not request that He preach them a sermon. They did not even ask Him to touch them. (He did touch them, but they did not request it.)

Salvation is not feelings. Salvation is not emotion. Salvation is not being faithful to the church Sunday after Sunday. We might sit under the sound of the gospel for a lifetime and hear the greatest preachers who have ever preached. We might sit in the class where the greatest Sunday school teacher on earth teaches; but that would not save us unless we individually believed that Jesus is able to do what the preacher is preaching and what the teacher is teaching *from God's Word.*

"Wherefore, HE IS ABLE also to save to the uttermost all who come unto God by him, seeing he ever liveth to make intercession for them" (Heb. 7:25). Paul believed and taught that Jesus is able to save to the uttermost — and may we add, *"to the guttermost."* He is able to save the most despicable man or woman in the gutter on the street of forgotten men and women. But He is just as able to save the banker, the doctor, the lawyer, the governor, the President, or "whosoever." His ability is not limited by our need. Regardless of how low one may have sunk in sin, Jesus is able to save to the uttermost; but that one must come unto God by Jesus. He is the only one who is able; He is the only one who has the power. He is the Way, the Truth, the Life, the Door. He is the SAVIOUR!

We have dealt with many people in inquiry rooms, in tents, tabernacles, churches, missions, jail houses and on street corners during the years of our ministry. Many times when a dear person has come to be saved, he has been instructed in the Scriptures, has bowed upon his knees and asked God to have mercy on him and save him. Yet when asked, "Now are you saved? Do you KNOW you are saved?" the answer often is, *"I am not sure."*

We then question in this manner: "Are you *sincere?* Did you really mean business when you came forward? Do you really *want* to be saved?" And the reply is, "YES! I am sincere! Yes, I DO want to be saved!"

When such a person in all sincerity seeks God — yet remains unsure as to whether God has saved him, such an attitude can mean but one thing: The sinner meant what HE said, but does not believe God meant what *He said!*

Jesus said, "Come unto me, I will give you rest" (Matt. 11:28-30).

"Come unto me. I will in no wise cast you out" (John 6:37).

"As many as received Him, to them gave he power to become the sons of God, even unto them that believe on his name" (John 1:12).

"By grace are ye saved through faith, and that not of yourselves. It is the gift of God, not of works..." (Eph. 2:8-9).

"Not by works of righteousness which we have done, but according to his mercy he has saved us by the washing of regeneration and the renewing of the Holy Ghost" (Titus 3:5).

"If we confess our sins, *he is faithful and just to forgive us our* sins and to cleanse us from all unrighteousness" (I John 1:9).

"Whosoever shall call upon the name of the Lord shall be saved" (Rom. 10:13).

When a person earnestly and sincerely repents of his sins and confesses those sins to God, and then says that he is not saved or that he is not sure he is saved, he is saying God lied, and dear friend, *God cannot lie!* To sum up the whole thing in a nutshell: You believe in your sincerity in your desire to be saved; *but you do not believe what God said in His Holy Word!*

We are saved by grace through faith (Eph. 2:8). Faith comes by hearing and hearing by the Word of God (Rom. 10:17). When you hear the Word of God and believe the Word of God, God saves you! And if you are not saved it is simply because you either do not want to be saved, or you do not believe God is able to do what He promises in His Word.

Hear these solemn words — and never doubt God's promises again: "In hope of eternal life, WHICH GOD, THAT CANNOT LIE, promised before the world began" (Titus 1:2). "That by two immutable things, in which IT WAS IMPOSSIBLE FOR GOD TO LIE, we might have a strong consolation, who have fled for refuge to lay hold upon the hope set before us, which hope we have as an anchor of the soul, both sure and steadfast" (Heb. 6:18-19a). "If we receive the witness of men, THE WITNESS OF GOD IS GREATER, for this is the witness of God which He hath testified of His Son: he that believeth on the Son of God HATH THE WITNESS IN HIMSELF: he that believeth not God HATH MADE HIM A LIAR; because he believeth not the record that God gave of his Son. And this is the record, that God hath given to us eternal life, AND THIS LIFE IS IN HIS SON. He that hath the Son hath life, and he that hath not the Son of God hath not life. These things have I written unto you that believe on the name of the Son of God; THAT YE MAY KNOW THAT YE HAVE

ETERNAL LIFE, and that ye may believe on the name of the Son of God (I John 5:9-13).

What Jesus actually said to the blind men was: "You have followed me this day with a desire in your heart to receive your sight. Down deep in your heart, do you really believe that I am able to open your eyes? Do you believe I have the power to remove the darkness and bring light to your eyes? Do you believe I am *able to do this?*"

"THIS"

When Jesus asked, "Do you believe I am able to do this," He was saying "Do you believe I can give you your eyesight?" Never having seen the light of day, they no doubt had heard of the miracles of Jesus. They probably had been told of other blind men who had had their sight restored by this great Teacher, and they wanted Jesus to do the same for them. Furthermore they believed *He was able* to do it.

What is the need in YOUR life? Do you believe Jesus is "able to do this?" Regardless of what your need may be, you may rest assured that God's Son IS able to meet that need. Jesus tells us that if we have faith as a grain of mustard seed, we can say to a mountain, "Be removed," and the mountain will be removed. "... And it shall remove and nothing shall be impossible unto you" (Matt. 17:20).

Jesus is able to save to the uttermost. He is able to "keep that which I have committed unto him against that day." He is able to deliver from all temptation, He is able to supply every need. He is able to go with us through the valley of the shadow of death, and He is able to stand with us when we stand before God. He is the only One to whom the Father will listen when our pleas are made. God saves sinners for Jesus' sake (Eph. 4:32).

Whatever "THIS" may be in your life, Jesus is able to meet that need. Do you believe this? Perhaps you have joined the church, been baptized, confirmed, dedicated, or christened when you were a baby; but do you need to be born again? Deep down in your heart, does your better self tell you that you need to be saved? Is salvation the *"this"* in your life? If it is, then do you believe Jesus is able to save you? Do you believe He is able to do it now?

Remember — God cannot lie. And "God so loved the world that he gave his only Begotten Son that whosoever" (that includes you) "believeth on him should not perish but have everlasting life." God has done everything He could do to keep you out of hell. God gave heaven's best, God permitted Jesus to die for you. And if you will receive Jesus now, He is able to save your soul. But "he that believeth not is condemned already BECAUSE *he hath not believed in the name of the only begotten Son of God*" (John 3:18). If you do not know that you are saved just as surely as you know you are breathing, bow your head and tell Jesus that you do believe He is able to save you. Then invite Him to come into your heart — and He will.

Perhaps you have been saved, but somewhere along the way, the devil caught you off guard and you became a backslider. I believe Peter was sincere when he said to Jesus, "All others may forsake you — but *you can count on me!* I will never deny you." Jesus told Peter that before the cock should crow, he would deny Him three times — and he did; but I still believe Peter was sincere. The devil caught him off guard and struck him in his spiritual weak spot. Peter denied his Lord — but he also went out and wept bitterly when he realized what he had done. You may be a backslider. You may be a Christian who has drifted away from the Lord. If that is your "this," Jesus is able to forgive your backsliding. He will — He desires to. God is married to the backslider.

David was a man after God's own heart. He sinned grievously, and it cost him a tremendous price — but God forgave him. Peter tells us that Lot was a just man, but he sinned against God and it cost him all that he had. God forgave Lot, just as Jesus forgave

Peter when he wept bitter tears of repentance. Peter later became one of the greatest preachers of the gospel.

Although you may be backslidden, Jesus loves you. He is willing, ready, and anxious to forgive your backsliding. He is able to do "this." These words are directed to the backslider: "My little children, these things write I unto you, that ye sin not. And if any man sin, we have an advocate with the Father, Jesus Christ the righteous: and he is the propitiation for our sins: and not for ours only, but also for the sins of the whole world" (I John 2:1-2).

If you have been genuinely born again and you have sinned against the Lord, Jesus is anxiously awaiting your return. Do it now. He is able — and not only able, He is anxious to forgive your backsliding and restore unto you the joy of your salvation.

Perhaps you need the victory over some habit. You are a Christian and you know beyond a shadow of a doubt that you are saved; but there are things in your life over which you do not have the victory. Perhaps you do things or go places that you know a Christian should not participate in. If that be the case, just remember, "There hath no temptation taken you but such as is common to man: but God is faithful, who will not suffer [permit] you to be tempted above that ye are able; but will with the temptation also make a way to escape, that ye may be able to bear it" (I Cor. 10:13).

There is victory in Jesus. You see, Jesus came into this world to take the sinner's place. Though tempted in all points as we are, He was without sin. He is able to deliver us out of temptation. As long as we are in the flesh, we will be tempted, tried and tested; but the Lord is able to deliver us. If your "this" is the need for victory over some habit that is robbing you of the joy of salvation, rest assured that Jesus is not only anxious, but He is also able, to give you grace to overcome that temptation, regardless of what it is. Commit it to Jesus, and He will give you victory.

There are many other things that we could discuss. Perhaps you need grace to love your neighbors. Perhaps you need grace to love those who persecute you. Perhaps you need grace to pray for them who despitefully use you. Maybe you need to be filled with the Spirit in order to be an effective soul-winner. Maybe you need the desire for Bible study planted in your heart. Regardless of what your "this" is, Jesus is able to supply it.

The conversation between Jesus and the two blind men took much less time than it has taken you to read this message. It opened with the request of the blind men: "Thou Son of David, have mercy on us." Then Jesus asked them, "Believe *YE* that *I* am able to do *this?*" The blind men answered in one accord: "Yea, Lord!" When they said "Yes, Lord, we believe you are able to do this," Jesus touched their eyes — and sight was miraculously there! But it was not the touch of Jesus that opened their eyes. They were just as blind the second after He touched them as they had been up to that moment. What made the difference was that Jesus touched their eyes, saying. "ACCORDING TO YOUR FAITH BE IT UNTO YOU."

Jesus had the ability, He had the power, to open their eyes; but it was their faith that made possible the miracle. Had they not been sincere and truthful from the heart when they said, "Yea, Lord," the touch of Jesus would have done them no good. They would have been just as blind after He touched them as they were before. But they were in earnest; they were sincere. They did tell the truth when they said, "Yea, Lord...Yes, we do believe that you are able to give us sight!" Such faith always brings a miracle — "AND THEIR EYES WERE OPENED."

Regardless of who you are, regardless of how sinful you are or how long you may have lived in sin, if you this moment with all of your heart will say to Jesus, "I believe you loved me and that you died to save me; I believe you are able to save sinners, I believe you WILL save me now...Come into my heart," I assure you that your blinded mind will be made to see, your dead spirit will be raised to newness of life and your crippled walk will be made straight.

All sinners are blind. All sinners are dead in trespasses and sins. All sinners are crippled by iniquity. Jesus is able to deliver immediately all who will have faith in His finished work.

"By grace are ye saved through faith, and that not of yourselves. It is the gift of God" (Eph. 2:8).

"So then faith cometh by hearing, and hearing by the word of God" (Rom. 10:17).

According to these two verses, salvation is God's gift, and God's gift becomes ours by faith. "Believe on the Lord Jesus Christ and thou shalt be saved" (Acts 16:31).

Believe YE that (*Jesus*) is able to do THIS?

Facts — Fears — Tears

Chapter IV

Facts — Fears — Tears

When liberals or modernists put question marks around Scripture, my answer always is "Let God be true, and every man a liar!" (Rom. 3:4). In this message we will discuss (1) Facts. (2) Fears. (3) Tears.

FACTS

"All we like sheep have gone astray" (Isa. 53:6a). Thus (spiritually speaking), Isaiah likens us to sheep and tells us we have *all gone astray;* there is no difference —we are all in the same category. Paul — called, ordained, and commissioned by God — expresses the same thought in these words:

"What then? are we better than they? No, in no wise: for we have before proved both Jews and Gentiles, that *they are all under sin;* As it is written, *There is none righteous, no, not one:* There is none that understandeth, there is none that seeketh after God. *They are all gone out of the way,* they are together become unprofitable; *there is none that doeth good, no, not one.* . . . for there is no difference: FOR ALL HAVE SINNED, AND

COME SHORT OF THE GLORY OF GOD" (Rom. 3:9-12; 22b; 23).

Here we have the Holy Spirit's word-picture of the unregenerate. We are born in sin, shapen in iniquity, and when we reach the age of accountability we are sinners — whether we be child of a preacher or of a bootlegger. After we reach the age of accountability, if we continue in sin we are then sinners by both nature and choice. God's grace takes care of the innocent, and no one can say when the age of accountability begins; but when one *reaches* that age, that one must be born again, regardless of who he is, regardless of the color of his skin or who his ancestors are. We are all in the same spiritual category in that respect.

There is a second fact found in Isaiah 53:6: "... The Lord [Jehovah God] hath laid on him [Jesus, the Lamb of God, Saviour of the world] the iniquity of us ALL."

It is a *fact* that we ALL have sinned.

It is a *fact* that we ALL have come short of the glory of God.

It is a *fact* that we ALL are like sheep, going astray.

But thank God for the *precious fact* that Jehovah God put our iniquities on Jesus and He carried our sins to the cross and nailed them there! "Who, HIS OWN SELF bare our sins in His own body on the tree, that we, being dead to sins, should live unto righteousness: BY WHOSE STRIPES YE WERE HEALED" (I Peter 2:24).

I have never found another verse of Scripture in the entire Bible exactly like Isaiah 53:6. The verse *begins* with "ALL" and *closes* with "ALL." All are in the same classification insofar as going away from God is concerned — but thank God, all can be in the same classification spiritually speaking if they will only believe on the Lord Jesus Christ and trust Him as Saviour.

This is also a fact: "If we say that we have no sin, we deceive ourselves, and the truth is not in us" (I John 1:8). We may deceive ourselves, we may tell ourselves that we are good, that we are not sinful, that we have done no wrong, that we have lived a good life all of our life; but we are deceiving no one but ourselves. God knows the thoughts and intents of the heart — He looks upon the heart, not on the outward appearance. It is not by works of righteousness which we have done that we are made fit for the kingdom of God, but according to HIS righteousness in Christ Jesus (Titus 3:5; II Cor. 5:21). If we tell ourselves that we do not need a Saviour, that we do not need repentance, that we do not need a blood-bought salvation, the Bible fact is that we are deceiving ourselves.

There is another glorious fact that immediately follows: "If we confess our sins, he is faithful and just to forgive us our sins, and to cleanse us from all unrighteousness" (I John 1:9). It does not matter what preachers preach, what teachers teach, nor what you read in a book. It is a Bible fact that if poor, lost sinners — sheep that have gone astray — shall *confess their sins,* God is faithful and just to *forgive* those sins, and to cleanse from ALL unrighteousness.

There are preachers and teachers who tell us that this is entirely too simple — too easy; but dearly beloved, it took Heaven's best to make this fact possible! It took the Lamb of God and His shed blood, together with everything He suffered, all the agony He endured. He paid sin's debt; He satisfied the heart of God; He is the Just One. If we confess our sins to Jesus, He is faithful, He will forgive and cleanse us, and make us righteous in God's sight.

It is a fact that *"the wages of sin is death."* These solemn words comprised the text the preacher used the night I was transformed from a wretched sinner into a son of the living God. That night, as I stood in the doorway of a little country church near Greenville, South Carolina, the minister proved to me from the Bible that my sin would damn me eternally in the lake of fire! He made the fact of sin so real, and its consequences so inescapable, I decided in my heart that it was time for me to do something about sin. He made the wages of sin so definite, and made it so clear that only the blood of Jesus would wash away my sin (Heb. 9:22; I John 1:7), that I put my trust in the shed blood of Jesus that night.

I did not — and I still do not — understand all about it; but I believed the fact that *"the wages of sin is death."* I believed the fact that *"the blood of Jesus Christ, God's Son, cleanses us from all sin."* I accepted the fact that *"without the shedding of blood is no remission of sin";* and then I heard the good news of God's gift to hell-deserving sinners: *Eternal life through Jesus Christ our Lord* (Rom. 6:23). I believed it, I received it, and *the fact of salvation* became mine that very night! From that night until this moment, I have never doubted that Jesus does exactly what His Word promises. I heard the Word, I received the Gift of God on the terms of the gospel — and God saved my soul for Jesus' sake (John 5:24; Eph. 4:32).

It is a fact that "When lust hath conceived it bringeth forth sin: and sin, when it is finished, bringeth forth death" (James 1:15). You do not need the Bible to prove the fact of *death*. Casket makers, grave diggers, and graveyards with their headstones can settle that fact apart from the Bible. It is a fact that the wages of sin is *death*, that when sin is finished it *"bringeth forth death";* but the sad fact is that *physical* death does not end it all: Eternal destruction awaits the unbeliever. Therefore, if you are not prepared to meet God, "make your calling and election sure." "TODAY is the day of salvation.... NOW is the accepted time.... Boast not thyself of tomorrow, for thou knowest not what a day may bring forth." *This moment is yours.* "Believe on the Lord Jesus Christ and thou shalt be saved!" (Acts 16:31).

FEARS

"Let us hear the conclusion of the whole matter: FEAR God, and keep his commandments: for this is the whole duty of man" (Eccl. 12:13). To be saved is a *glorious opportunity*. To live for

Jesus is a glorious *privilege;* but to fear God and keep His commandments is the *duty* of man. Along with the privilege of being a Christian, we have the command from Almighty God to fear Him and keep His commandments.

Perhaps someone is saying, "You ministers preach that we are born in sin and are sinners by nature. If that be true, why should I suffer for Adam's sin?" I answer with Romans 9:20: "Nay but, O man, WHO ART THOU THAT REPLIEST AGAINST GOD? Shall the thing formed say to him that formed it, Why hast thou made me thus?"

It is true that through the disobedience of one man, sin moved upon *all* men — and death by sin; but it is also true that God has made provision for all sin and for all sinners. It is not God's will that any sinner perish. Therefore, since God has provided salvation for all — free, understandable, obtainable by simply trusting in the finished work of Jesus — "O man, *who art thou that repliest against God?*" God has provided redemption for the soul and spirit. He will give us a glorified body when we shall reach that city, and He has made provision to take care of us *until* that time — soul, spirit, and body. He has promised grace sufficient for every trial; victory over every temptation; and food and raiment until we reach Home (I Cor. 10:13; Matt. 6:33; II Cor. 12:9; Heb. 13:5-6; Phil. 4:19).

Sermons that produce fear have been almost outlawed from the pulpits of today; but I do not believe there has ever been a case of genuine repentance toward God that was not preceded by fear. I can prove that statement from God's Holy Word:

"By faith Noah, being warned of God of things not seen as yet, MOVED WITH FEAR, prepared an ark to the saving of his house; by the which he condemned the world, and became heir of the righteousness which is by faith" (Heb. 11:7).

Noah was the only person alive in his day who believed God's Word. God announced that a flood would be sent upon the earth, by way of judgment, and Noah believed what God said.

"Faith cometh by hearing, and hearing by the Word of God" (Rom. 10:17). God instructed Noah to build an ark and Noah built it exactly according to God's blueprint. When it was finished, God came down, inspected the ark, and said to Noah: "Come thou, and all thy house, into the ark."

Why did Noah build an ark? Why did he labor through those discouraging years? If anyone helped him the Scriptures do not reveal it. His sons probably helped, but outside of his own family, he *had* no help. Why did he build the ark? God never came down to inspect the progress of the work, and Noah never received a paycheck...but he kept on building. Why? *Because he believed God.*

Noah was warned of God concerning things he had never seen. Prior to the flood, rain had never fallen upon the earth. Until that time, a mist came up from the ground each night and watered the earth with dew. There had never been a thundercloud, nor had a drop of water ever fallen from the sky until Noah was safe within the ark. God warned him that He would send rain, and water would cover the highest mountains the world over. The message moved Noah WITH FEAR. He immediately set about to prepare an ark according to God's directions. He saved his house, condemned the world — and became the heir of righteousness BY FAITH.

Mark 5:24-34 tells of a woman "which had an issue of blood for twelve years." She was part of the great crowd that followed Jesus, and as the multitude pressed around Him, Jesus suddenly asked, *"Who touched my clothes?"* The disciples mildly reproved Him, reminding Him that He was thronged with people — and yet He had asked, "Who touched me?"

Jesus knew that someone had touched Him with the touch of faith. "But the woman, FEARING AND TREMBLING, knowing what was done in her, came and fell down before Him, and told Him all the truth" (Mark 5:33). A miracle was worked in the body of this dear woman. She had spent all of her living and was none the better. The issue of blood had continued for twelve years — until she touched Jesus in fear and trembling — and was instantly healed!

In the twenty-third chapter of Luke we read that as Jesus hung on the cross between two thieves, the multitude around the crosses laughed, jeered, sneered, and mocked Him. At first the two thieves "cast the same in His teeth," but a little later in the day one of the thieves changed his mind about the Man on the middle cross. Perhaps this thief had listened to the words of Jesus as He prayed. "Father, forgive them ... they know not what they do." Perhaps he saw something in the face of the suffering Saviour which convinced him that Jesus was more than an ordinary man, and caused him to say to the other thief, "DOST NOT THOU FEAR GOD, seeing thou art in the same condemnation? And we indeed justly; for we receive the due reward of our deeds: but this man hath done nothing amiss. And he said unto Jesus, *Lord, remember me when thou comest into thy kingdom.* And Jesus said unto him, Verily I say unto thee, Today shalt thou be with me in paradise" (Luke 23:39-43). Something created *fear* in the heart of the dying thief. In fear he looked at Jesus and said, "LORD, remember me!" Jesus took him to Paradise that day.

I repeat — I do not believe there has ever been a real, genuine case of repentance toward God that was not preceded by godly fear.

In Mark 15:39 we find another scene at the crucifixion. As Jesus hung on the cross, the centurion had taken his place "over against Jesus." Standing there, he saw and heard the howling, mocking throng. He witnessed the entire, agonizing crucifixion. When Jesus cried out with a loud voice and gave up the ghost, something happened in the heart of the centurion: "Now when the centurion, and they that were with him, watching Jesus, saw the earthquake, and those things that were done, *they feared greatly,* saying, Truly this was the Son of God" (Matt. 27:54).

"Jesus cried with a loud voice." No doubt this helped to convince the centurion that he had witnessed the death of the Son of God. A bleeding, dying person does not scream nor cry with a loud voice. A dying man who has been bleeding and under torture for hours speaks in a whisper or a groan. When Jesus "cried with a loud voice," He literally passed His life back to God. The moment He said "Father, into thy hands I commend my Spirit," His head fell limp on His pulseless breast and His body hung lifeless on the cross.

The centurion, seeing and hearing these things, FEARED GREATLY. He then confessed, "Truly, *this Man was the Son of God!*" That confession was his salvation.

The verse that changed *me* from a drunk to a son of God was Romans 10:9: "That if thou shalt confess with thy mouth the Lord Jesus, and shalt believe in thine heart that God hath raised him from the dead, thou shalt be saved." I did that — and God saved me. The centurion did it — and I expect to meet him in Heaven. But notice — before he confessed that he had witnessed the death of the Son of God, he *"feared greatly."*

Another instance of sincere repentance preceded by godly fear is given in Acts 16. Paul and Silas were preaching in Philippi, and for several days they had been consistently followed by a demon-possessed fortune teller. "...Paul, being grieved, turned and said to the spirit, I command thee in the name of Jesus Christ to come out of her! And he came out the same hour"(Acts 16:18b). When this girl was converted, her masters saw that the hope of their gains was gone. In anger they "caught Paul and Silas, and drew them into the marketplace unto the rulers, and brought them to the magistrates, saying, These men, being Jews, do exceedingly trouble our city."

As a result of the charges brought against them, Paul and Silas were beaten, "and when they had laid many stripes upon them, they cast them into prison, charging the jailer to keep them safely." Having received his charge, the jailer thrust his prisoners

into the inner prison [the dungeon] and made their feet fast in
the stocks. And at midnight — bleeding, cold, hungry, tired, Paul
and Silas "prayed and sang praises unto God!"

God said "AMEN!" with an earthquake that shook the very
foundations of the prison, and burst open every door. All fetters
and chains, stocks and bonds were broken, and every prisoner
was set free! The keeper of the prison awakened out of his sleep,
saw the prison doors open and the prisoners walking freely about.

According to the law in Philippi, if a jailer allowed a prisoner
to escape, he forfeited his own life as penalty. The Philippian
jailer knew that law, and rather than face the executioner *"he
drew out his sword, and would have killed himself, supposing
that the prisoners had been fled"* (Acts 16:27).

But Paul cried "with a loud voice; saying, *Do thyself no harm!*
We are all here! No one has gone anywhere. Don't kill yourself
... don't take a short cut to hell. Put up your sword!"

The Scripture tells us that the jailer called for a light, *"and
sprang in."* The Philippian jailer presents a marked contrast to
some of the people I have seen come forward in meetings. Sometimes I am compelled to wonder, "Do you really mean business?"
People come down the aisle with heavy feet, so much as if to
say, "I am going to trust Jesus — but it is certainly a sacrifice to
leave the pleasures of the world and embrace Christianity!" Such
a reluctant attitude causes me to wonder if these people are
really saved. They may join the church — but that is not
salvation.

The jailer SPRANG (literally jumped) in, *trembling, and fell
down before Paul and Silas.* This is a far cry from some of the
dignified altar calls in our churches today, when the lovely minister finishes his Sunday morning essay and invites his congrega-
tion, "If any of you lovely people would like to unite with our
lovely church, walk down the aisle and place your lovely hand
in my lovely hand." God help us to get back to dogmatic

preaching! God help us never to apologize for asking a soul to stay out of hell!

The Philippian jailer "sprang in, and came trembling, and fell down before Paul and Silas," and his all-important question was, "Sirs, WHAT MUST I DO TO BE SAVED?" He did not ask, "What must I do to become a member of the temple in Jerusalem?" nor, "What must I do to become a member of your religious group...how can I join your fellowship?" The jailer knew he was in the presence of God's messengers, and simply said, "Sirs, I want to be saved. Tell me how!"

They did! Paul and Silas were agreed on this. I wish preachers were agreed today on such matters. *They* said, *"Believe on the Lord Jesus Christ and thou shalt be saved, and thy house!"* Faith comes by hearing and hearing by the Word. Paul and Silas "spake unto him the word of the Lord, and to all that were in his house." We are not born again of corruptible seed, but incorruptible — by the Word. *"He that heareth my word and believeth on him that sent me hath everlasting life."* Paul and Silas were efficient soul winners. They preached the Word of God — and the jailer and all of his household were saved and baptized. They prepared a delicious meal for God's ministers; they ate and rejoiced, *"believing in God with all his house"* (Acts 16:34).

The poor, pagan jailer at Philippi feared, trembled, fell upon his knees — *and was saved.* I am not saying that every person who is born again should fall upon his knees, or tremble at the feet of a preacher; I am simply reaffirming that there has never been a case of genuine repentance toward God that was not *preceded by godly fear*: "The fear of the Lord is the *beginning* of knowledge" (Prov. 1:7a).

Individuals demonstrate fear in different ways; some tremble, while others may show no outward sign of inward distress. Godly fear is a thing of the heart, and unless we fear God, we will never ask Him to have mercy on us as sinners. We will never see the need of a Saviour until we fear the judgment of Almighty God and the punishment of an eternal hell.

When YOU "got religion," what happened to you? Did you have a genuine experience with God? or did you just shake the preacher's hand, fill out a card, and sign a pledge? Think it over. In the words of Jesus, "Except a man be born again he cannot see the kingdom of God" (John 3:5).

TEARS

I would not say that all true conversions are either preceded or followed by tears, but God honors a broken and contrite heart (Ps. 51:17); and tears *denote* a broken heart.

"...Christ glorified not himself to be made an high priest; but he that said unto him, Thou art my Son, today have I begotten thee. As he saith also in another place, Thou art a priest for ever after the order of Melchisedec. Who in the days of his flesh, when he had offered up prayers and supplications with strong crying and tears unto him that was able to save him from death, and was heard in that he feared" (Heb. 5:5-7).

These solemn words refer to our Lord, the Lamb of God upon whom all iniquity was placed — the One who bore our sins and carried our sorrows. He was wounded for our transgressions. He was bruised for our iniquities, the chastisement of our peace was upon Him — and only with His stripes can we be healed. He was smitten of God, He feared, He wept WITH STRONG CRYING AND TEARS.

I firmly believe one of the great needs in the church today is more broken hearts. We need less laughter and more weeping; less light preaching and more preaching that breaks the heart and produces bitter tears.

One of the most touching accounts in the Word of God concerning the public ministry of Jesus is that given in Luke 7:36-50. After conducting a street meeting, Jesus went to the house of Simon the Pharisee for dinner. In the shadows stood a woman, hidden from the crowd but hearing the words of Jesus; and those words broke her sinful heart.

As Jesus sat at meat in the house of the Pharisee, this woman came with an alabaster box of ointment. She did not ask if she might enter — had she knocked at the door she would not have been allowed inside. She was a sinner whose life was known by everyone, and she dared not ask to be admitted to the presence of Jesus. She entered unannounced and stood at His feet — weeping. She began to wash His feet with her tears and to wipe them with the hairs of her head. She kissed His feet and anointed them with ointment (Luke 7:38).

This was most unusual. Perhaps no other man has had his feet bathed with the tears of a broken hearted woman. Perhaps no other man has had his feet dried with the hair of a woman's head. Jesus is perhaps the only person who ever had his feet covered with kisses from a woman's lips. Then she broke the alabaster box and anointed His feet with precious ointment.

Simon the Pharisee was a religious man. He knew the woman was a great sinner, and he said, "This man, *if he were a prophet,* would have known who and what manner of woman this is that toucheth him: for she is a sinner" (Luke 7:39).

Jesus said to Simon, "I entered into your house and you gave me no water to wash my feet — but this woman has washed them with tears and wiped them with the hairs of her head. You gave me no kiss — but she has not ceased to kiss my feet. You did not anoint my head with oil — but this woman has anointed my feet with costly ointment. Wherefore I say unto thee, Her sins, which are many, are forgiven; for she loved much: but to whom little is forgiven, the same loveth little."

To the woman, Jesus said, "Thy sins are forgiven ... thy faith hath saved thee. Go in peace" (Luke 7:44-50 in part).

It was not her tears that saved her, nor was it the wiping of His feet with her hair nor yet the ointment with which she anointed His feet. Jesus said, "Thy FAITH hath saved thee," but *the faith she had in her heart was demonstrated* through her tears and her loving service to Her Lord. *Faith without works is dead.* She proved her faith by what she did. She wept in repentance, she worked in loving service, she gave the best she had to Jesus.

Where did she get this faith? She listened to the message of Jesus before He went into Simon's house! We are saved by grace through faith (Eph. 2:8). Faith comes by hearing, and hearing by the Word of God (Rom. 10:17). In John 5:24 we have enough gospel to save the world — if the world would only believe!

————

The twenty-second chapter of Luke gives us the picture of a rough, ruddy, seasoned veteran of the nets, bowed with grief while tears rolled down his cheeks. After the institution of the Lord's supper, Jesus went to the Garden of Gethsemane to pray. Peter, James, and John went with Him, and while they were there, Judas came with a band of soldiers to arrest Jesus. Judas betrayed the Lord with a kiss, the soldiers arrested Him and led Him away — *"And Peter followed afar off"* (Luke 22:54).

When the enemies of Jesus kindled a fire in the courtyard before the house of the high priest, "Peter sat down among them." A little maid, seeing him, said, "This man also was with Him." Peter denied Him (Jesus), saying, "Woman, I know Him not!" He continued to sit and warm himself, and after a little while another said, "Thou art also of them." Again Peter said, *"Man, I am not!"* After the space of about an hour, another declared, "Of a truth this fellow also was with Him: for he is a Galilean" (Luke 22:59).

Poor Peter! He was warm now — but his warmth had come from the devil's fire, kindled by the enemies of Jesus. In reply to this last accusation, he swore an oath and vehemently said, "Man, I know not what thou sayest!" No sooner had the words left

Peter's lips than the cock crew, and with the crowing of the cock *Peter remembered.* "AND THE LORD TURNED AND LOOKED UPON PETER." When Peter saw the face of Jesus, when his eyes met the loving, compassionate eyes of his Lord gazing sadly upon him as he warmed himself by the devil's fire, it broke his heart! He was fellowshipping with God's enemies, he had denied his Lord three times. When his eyes met the eyes of Jesus, he *"remembered the word of the Lord."*

Earlier that evening, Jesus had told Peter that before the cock crew, he (Peter) would thrice deny Him. Faith comes by hearing—and hearing by the Word of God (Rom. 10:17). The Word is the power of God unto salvation (Rom. 1:16). We are born again through the Word (I Peter 1:23). Peter remembered the Word— and what happened?

"PETER WENT OUT AND WEPT BITTERLY!" (Luke 22:62). A hard, rough, brawny, red-faced fisherman melted into tears when his eyes met those of the loving Christ. Peter separated himself from the company of the enemies of Jesus, left the warmth of the fire kindled by the devil's crowd, and went out into the cold night, to fall upon his knees and weep bitter tears of repentance.

———

In Hebrews 12:14-47 we read, "Follow peace with all men, and holiness, without which no man shall see the Lord: Looking diligently lest any man fail of the grace of God; lest any root of bitterness springing up trouble you, and thereby many be defiled; lest there be any fornicator, or profane person, as Esau, who for one morsel of meat sold his birthright. For ye know how that afterward, when he would have inherited the blessing, he was rejected: for he found no place of repentance, *though he sought it carefully with tears.*"

Poor Esau! He sold his birthright for a morsel of meat.

Poor Judas! He sold his Lord for the price of a slave.

Poor sinners today! Selling their spiritual birthright for some frivolity, some worldly pleasure, some worthless trinket.

Dear friend, what is the price tag hell has hung on your soul? Whatever it is, it is not worth the price. Believe the Bible fact: "All have sinned." Then believe the second part of that great verse: "God hath laid on Him [Jesus] the iniquity of us all!" Believe those two facts — *and fear God with all of your heart.* Come to Him in fear, believe on Him in faith, serve Him in love, and trust Him with all of your heart. If you do that, unless I miss my guess you, too, will feel the warmth of tears trickling down your cheeks.

No — tears will not save you; but tears do advertise a broken and contrite heart. It is a fact that we must die, we must face God, we must be judged in righteousness. Therefore, fear God and keep His commandments, for this is the whole duty of man. God created us, and it is our duty to do what our Creator commands.

Weep, repent with strong tears, lay your burden before the Lord, and He will take your burden. Today is the day of salvation, now is the accepted time. "Boast not thyself of tomorrow.... Believe on the Lord Jesus Christ, and thou shalt be saved!"

Desire — Decision — Disaster

Chapter V

Desire — Decision — Disaster

The Bible is one book. All of its sixty-six books make *one book*, with *one primary message*. Centuries ago the gospel was the same as it is today. The Bible is a book of dispensational truth, but regardless of the dispensation, salvation is and always has been entirely God's gift to unworthy sinners — God's mercy, extended to us who do not deserve mercy.

There are three passages in God's Holy Word which convey exactly the same message (expressed in different words) — yet this message was given to Holy men of old — men who lived *centuries apart*. God is one God, and He changes not (Heb. 13:8).

In the first chapter of Isaiah, Jehovah presents His case against Judah: "I have nourished and brought up children, and they have rebelled against me.... Ah sinful nation, a people laden with iniquity, a seed of evildoers... *Hear the Word of the Lord,* ye rulers.... *give ear unto the law of our God,* ye people....To what purpose is the multitude of your sacrifices unto me?....I am full of the burnt offerings of rams, and the fat of fed beasts;

and I delight not in the blood of bullocks, or of lambs, or of he goats.

"When ye come to appear before me, who hath required this at your hand, to tread my courts? Bring no more vain oblations; incense is an abomination unto me; the new moons and sabbaths, the calling of assemblies, I cannot away with; it is iniquity, even the solemn meeting. Your new moons and your appointed feasts my soul hateth: they are a trouble unto me; I am weary to bear them. And when ye spread forth your hands, I will hide mine eyes from you: yea, when ye make many prayers, I will not hear: your hands are full of blood. Wash ye, make you clean; put away the evil of your doings from before mine eyes; cease to do evil; Learn to do well; seek judgment, relieve the oppressed, judge the fatherless, plead for the widow. COME NOW, AND LET US REASON TOGETHER, SAITH THE LORD: *though your sins be as scarlet,* they shall be as *white as snow;* though they be red like crimson, they shall be as wool. IF YE BE WILLING AND OBEDIENT, ye shall eat of the good of the land: BUT IF YE REFUSE AND REBEL, ye shall be devoured with the sword: for the mouth of the Lord hath spoken it" (Isa. 1:1-24 in part).

The prophet Isaiah stood silent beside the bedside of the dying king. Isaiah was very sad, his soul was stirred — and in later days he wrote, *"In the year that King Uzziah died,* I saw also the Lord sitting upon a throne, high and lifted up.... Also I heard the voice of the Lord, saying, Whom shall I send, and who will go for us? Then said I, Here am I; send me. And he said, Go" (Isa. 6:1-8).

Thus Isaiah received his commission from Almighty God, and went forth to preach. In his preaching he declared the message God had given him. If we carefully study the entire book of Isaiah, we find that his message to Judah contained three major points, the first of which was

DESIRE

God revealed to Isaiah that He longed to meet the need of His people. His desire was to pardon their sins, forgive their iniquities, wash them as white as snow. He desired to give them peace within their hearts. After sternly rebuking Judah, God declared that "an ox knoweth his owner, and an ass his master's crib, but Israel doth not know, my people do not consider." (That is one way of saying that Israel was more ignorant than a dumb ox or an ass.)

In spite of the rebuke He had given, God — with a heart of compassion, tenderness, and longsuffering — sent His people this invitation: "Come now! Come unto me. I have a deep desire to reason with you. It is true that your sins are as scarlet...they are red like crimson. But my desire is to wash your sins away and make them as white as the snow!"

God had the desire. He longed to forgive Israel, to take His people in his arms and kiss away their guilt. He desired to blot out their transgressions and wash their hearts and lives as white as the driven snow...but it was up to His people to make the

DECISION

Judah decided against the invitation. God said, "Come now ...I am ready to reason with you, I am anxious to wash away your scarlet sins and make them as wool... *if ye be willing and obedient.* But if you are not willing, if you do not obey, *if ye refuse and rebel,* ye shall be devoured with the sword!"

God's gracious offer was rejected: "In returning and rest shall ye be saved; in quietness and in confidence shall be your strength: AND YE WOULD NOT. But ye said, NO, FOR WE WILL FLEE UPON HORSES; therefore shall ye flee: and, We will ride upon the swift; therefore shall they that pursue you be swift" (Isa. 30:15-16).

God had the desire to save His people. He gave the invitation. But it was up to Judah to make the decision, and they decided that they would not return. They said "No!" to God's invitation.

These people were like their children of a later century, when Pilate asked, "What then shall I do with your King?" and they replied, "Crucify Him! Let His blood be upon us and upon our children!" In Isaiah's day the people preferred their own way of life. They willfully indulged in sin. They found great joy in the pleasures of the flesh. They did not want their scarlet sins washed away. They enjoyed the things of the devil. They said to God, *"We will not return.* Our answer to your invitation is, No!" Such a reply left God no alternative but

DISASTER

When God calls and men refuse; when He stretches out His hand and men pay no attention; when men set at nought His counsel and refuse to listen to His reproof — then God declares, "I will laugh at your calamity; I will mock when your fear cometh" (Prov. 1:22, 23).

"The wages of sin is death" in any era. Since Judah said "No" to God, He was forced to give unto them "the bread of adversity and the water of affliction." Oh yes — it is true that they eventually returned to Palestine — but not until after they had suffered many years of trials and tribulations — *and they left many graves in Babylon!*

"Be not deceived, God is not mocked." Whatsoever a nation sows, that nation must reap — whether it be Israel or America. Seed sown will inevitably produce a harvest. There is no way to escape the harvest of destruction if we make a decision against God's desire to be our God and direct our paths.

———

In Genesis 3:15 God promised the Saviour. Centuries later, Jesus came as promised — born of a virgin. Step by step the prophecies concerning His birth were fulfilled. Someone has said, "It seems incredible that Judah could have missed her Mes-

siah, Jesus was born with so many labels on Him." Everything
the Old Testament said about His birth was literally fulfilled —
and yet, "He came unto His own, and His own received Him
not!" Jesus was God in flesh — yet He was as human as you and
I. He loved His brethren; He loved the home of Lazarus; He
loved to go to the mountains to pray — and I am sure He loved
to sit in Peter's fishing boat on the Sea of Galilee.

He loved the Holy City where the temple was. Sitting on the
Mount of Olives, with His eyes fastened lovingly upon that city
in the Judaean hills, sorrow filled His heart and grief gripped
His spirit. Just across the way was the garden tomb of Joseph of
Arimathea, which tomb Jesus knew He was soon to occupy. He
had come for the last time to the city He loved.

Looking out over Jerusalem, He could see the people as they
moved through the narrow streets. He could see the little don-
keys laden with merchandise. Burdened under His overwhelming
love for His people, He wept over them.

DESIRE

Jesus cried out: "O Jerusalem, Jerusalem, thou that killest the
prophets, and stonest them which are sent unto thee, how often
would I have gathered thy children together even as a hen
gathereth her chickens under her wings, AND YE WOULD
NOT! Behold, your house IS LEFT unto you desolate. For I
say unto you, Ye shall not see me henceforth, till ye shall say,
Blessed is he that cometh in the name of the Lord" (Matt.
23:37-39).

What deep longing, what burning desire, is seen in the words,
"O, Jerusalem! Jerusalem! How often would I have gathered thy
children together, as a hen gathereth her chickens under her
wings!" He came unto His own — His own brethren — the seed
of Abraham — and His own received Him not, in spite of His
desire.

The fact that Jesus said "... how often..." signifies that this was not the only time He desired to save His people. It would indicate that many times He had looked upon His own and had been moved with compassion. He saw the fields white unto harvest, the multitudes as sheep without a shepherd. He desired to gather them unto Himself as a mother hen gathers her chickens under her wings to protect them from enemies and the elements that would destroy them.

The Greatest Teacher and Greatest Preacher who ever lived used illustrations that even a child could easily understand. Study the sermons of Jesus and you will find that His messages were simple, direct, and down to earth where people live. He talked about the sower and the seed . . . the wheat and tares that grew together until harvest. He talked of the sheep and the goats . . . the sparrows . . . the lilies of the field — and when He wanted to drive home the fact that man is frail and mortal He said, *"All flesh is as grass!"* Jesus preached simple, yet profound sermons, in language easily understood. One of the greatest needs in the pulpits of today is for God's preachers to come back down to earth. We are dealing with earthly people who need a Saviour, and we need to deliver messages that can be easily understood, even by a child. Jesus had the desire to save His people — but *they* made the

DECISION

The sad words, ". . . and ye would not!" sum up the decision of the Jews. They were God's elect, God's chosen — and yet — "His own received Him not." Instead, they said, "We will not have this man to reign over us!" To Jesus they said, *"We know who you are!* We know your father, we know your mother. You are an impostor!" In their rage against Him they cried out, "Crucify Him! Let his blood be upon us and upon our children." *They made the decision.*

Jesus so longed to save them. He longed to shelter them — but they cried, "Give us Barabbas! We had rather be robbed —

we had rather have a murderer in our midst. We do not want this Nazarene! Let him be crucified!" They demanded His death, and Pilate turned Him over to the Jews at their demand. They nailed Him to a cross — and mocked Him while He died!

The Saviour had the desire to gather His people unto Himself as a hen gathers her chickens under her wings when danger threatens. Judah made the decision, they chose a murderer instead of Jesus. Therefore, God had no alternative except

DISASTER

"Behold, your house is left unto you desolate!" Please notice the little word "is." These words were spoken before Jesus was crucified. At that moment the houses were standing, and the people were busy in the shops and in the fields. Yet Jesus said, "Your house IS left unto you desolate" — not *going to be*, not in the future — but NOW! You have made your decision; you have rejected your Saviour. You did not want the lowly Nazarene. Your great prophet Isaiah told you the Lamb would come; you read of me in Zechariah; yet you did not recognize me as Messiah when I came . . . you did not receive me."

There is such a thing as crossing God's deadline — for an individual, a home, or a nation. Man can ignore God and get away with it for a season; but "he that being often reproved hardeneth his neck, shall be suddenly cut off and that without remedy." When men know God, but refuse to glorify Him AS God; when men change the truth of God into a lie and worship and serve the creature more than the Creator; when men do not like to retain God in their knowledge — *God gives them up* (Rom. 1:18 ff). Judah had known God, had walked with Him, and communed with Him. They were God's elect. He had given them the prophecy concerning the coming of their Messiah — yet when He came, they received Him not. They demanded His death. That moment, Jehovah God wrote "Finished!" across their record, "Doomed!" across their destiny — and gave them up to destruction.

In A.D. 70 Titus the Roman ruler butchered five million Jews in Jerusalem in one day, and leveled the city! That is perhaps the greatest human slaughter in one day — and consider that Titus had neither guided missiles, atomic bombs, nor jet bombers. He did not have the gas chambers of Hitler in World War II. He *butchered his victims with the sword!* They had asked for it when they said, "Let His blood be upon us. . . . !"

Eichman was tried, convicted, and hanged for killing six million Jews. I do not doubt his guilt; but the Jews brought such destruction upon themselves 1900 years ago when they shouted, "Crucify Him! We had rather be robbed and murdered than have Him as King!" Beloved, if God be for us, who can be against us? (Rom. 8:31). But if God is against us, we ARE destroyed — *present tense.* Apart from God there is no hope.

God has the desire to save "whosoever will." He sent Jesus, gave His only begotten Son, "that *whosoever believeth* in Him should not perish, but have everlasting life." God desires to save *all* . . . it is not His will that any should perish, but that all should come to repentance (II Peter 3:9). God wants to save from the "guttermost" to the uttermost — but if you decide you do not want Jesus and salvation, then God cannot save you. God is love, and love does not use force. God is not a dictator. He loves you, He desires to save you — but if you decide against Him, He has no alternative but to bring judgment upon you, because God "will not at all acquit the wicked" (Nahum 1:3).

"The wages of sin is death" (Rom. 6:23). "The soul that sinneth, it shall die" (Ezek. 18:4). When men decide to serve sin instead of serving God, they must be destroyed eternally in the lake of fire.

———

Jesus often taught in parables, using them to illustrate spiritual truths. One of the greatest of His parables was that of the marriage feast, as recorded in Matthew 22:1-10: "And Jesus answered and spake unto them again by parables, and said, The Kingdom of Heaven is like unto a certain king, which made a marriage for His son, and sent forth his servants to call them that were bidden to the wedding: and they would not come. Again, He sent forth other servants, saying, Tell them which are bidden, Behold I have prepared my dinner: my oxen and my fatlings are killed, and all things are ready: come unto the marriage. But they made light of it, and went their ways, one to his farm, another to his merchandise. And the remnant took his servants, and entreated them spitefully, and slew them. But when the king heard thereof, he was wroth: and he sent forth his armies, and destroyed those murderers, and burned up their city. Then saith he to his servants, The wedding is ready, but they which were bidden were not worthy. Go ye therefore into the highways, and as many as ye shall find, bid to the marriage. So those servants went out into the highways, and gathered together all as many as they found, both bad and good: and the wedding was furnished with guests."

The king's palace was filled with excitement — the Prince was to be married! And the king sent forth his servants to call them *that were bidden* to the wedding. (The invitations had been prepared and sent out days ahead, to notify friends that the wedding was to be.) When the day of the wedding arrived, the king sent servants throughout the village to personally remind those who had received invitations, that the day of the marriage had arrived. The king desired the company of his neighbors and friends at the marriage of his son. HE was the one who prepared the feast; HE furnished the fatlings; HIS cooks prepared the food; HE paid the bills; HE sent out the invitations; HE had

GREAT DESIRE

The king left no stone unturned to do everything in his power to make the wedding of his son a most gala event. He spared neither money, time, nor effort. "ALL things are ready." Nothing was overlooked — every detail was taken care of. All the guests need do was simply *come*. They need not bring money, food, nor robes — just themselves. The king desired their company. His son was to be married. Strange as it may seem, the king's neighbors and friends decided against attending the weding feast. They made their own

DECISION

"And they would not come!" The servants carried the message, "ALL things are ready. The fatlings are killed, the food is prepared, the table is set. COME!" But they would not come.

The king did not give up: "Again he sent forth other servants." This time, they not only refused to come to the feast — *they made light of the king*. They mocked and made fun. One went to his farm, another to his merchandise. Others went their own way — and those who remained took the servants, "entreated them spitefully," and killed them!

These people had "a second chance." How many chances have YOU had, dear friend, if you are not saved? Many times I have bowed my head and given thanks to God for the many chances He gave me. Again and again I said "No" to God — but He spared me until that glad hour when I heard the invitation, "Come — All things are ready. Come — I will in no wise cast you out. Come unto me — I will give you rest" (Matt. 11:28; John 6:37). I will never cease to praise God that He spared me and let me live until I came to myself, heard the call of God, and surrendered my heart and life to Jesus!

(Let me make it very clear that I do not believe there is a second chance after death. When you close your eyes in death, your destiny is eternally fixed. If you die in your sins, you will spend eternity in hell. If you die in the Lord you will spend eternity with Jesus.)

The king in our parable had a deep, sincere desire. He sent

two groups of servants to carry the good news that the wedding feast was ready. But his neighbors and friends decided against it. They would not come, they made fun of the king, went their own way — and even slew his servants! That left the king no choice other than

DISASTER

In A.D. 70 when Titus overran Jerusalem, this parable was literally fulfilled. There were five million Jews butchered in one day, their houses throughout the city were burned, the city walls were leveled — not one stone left upon another. Jesus prophesied it in John 2:19 and Matthew 24:1-2.

The king in this parable represents God the Father; the son represents the Lord Jesus Christ. The servants represent the disciples, ministers and missionaries of today.

The King furnished everything for the feast; He *desired* the fellowship of His brethren, friends, and neighbors. His friends and neighbors made the *decision* — they would not come! They made light of the invitation, went their separate ways — and *disaster befell them!*

"But when the King heard thereof, *he was wroth*: And he sent forth his armies, and destroyed those murderers, and burned up their city!" Swift, horrible, total destruction! Why? Because those people decided against the king's desire for their company at the marriage of his son.

That does not sound like the lovely, tender, grandfatherly God the modernists and liberals talk about today, does it? They preach "the fatherhood of God, the brotherhood of man, everyone is good, no one is bad. We just need to educate the people, polish the preachers, and destroy the slums!" No, our parable does not sound like the message of Dr. Sounding Brass or Professor Tinkling Cymbal. From Genesis to Revelation, the precious Bible clearly teaches that "God is angry with the wicked every day." The fury of God will be poured out upon the ungodly.

It is appointed unto men once to die, and after death, the judgment. I ask you in Bible language, What shall it profit ANY man — even you or me — if he gain the whole world, become dictator of this earth, and lose his soul? In the sight of God, one soul is more valuable than all the wealth of all the world.

God's Son left the Father's bosom because *the Father* desired to save sinners. Jesus left Heaven's glory because *He* desired to pay sin's debt and purchase redemption for you and me. God gave Heaven's best — He went the limit so deeply did He desire that you and I miss hell! But if you decide that you do not *want* Jesus as your Saviour, then God can do nothing to help you. The only way God can save you is "for Jesus' sake." What God does for the sinner He does because of Jesus and His shed blood. God loved us, and gave Jesus who took the sinner's place. The only way a sinner can approach God is in the name of Jesus, through the shed blood of His cross. And if we decide against Jesus, God has no alternative. He MUST destroy us — *and He will!*

One glad and glorious day, evil will be put down, Lucifer will be put into the lake of fire and brimstone, and the knowledge of the Lord will cover the earth. "The meek shall inherit the earth and delight themselves in the abundance of peace." There *will be* peace on earth and good will toward men — but not until King Jesus sits on the throne of His father, David. Not until that grand and glorious time when the church has been caught up to meet Jesus in the clouds in the air, a marriage takes place as the church is married to the Bridegroom, and together we return to this earth to reign for one thousand glorious years. But beloved — you may rest assured that before that day comes, Antichrist and his murderers will be destroyed. God is love, God is longsuffering. God is good — but God is also a consuming fire and He will judge wickedness in righteous judgment.

"There is a way which seemeth right unto a man, but the end thereof are the ways of death" (Prov. 14:12).

In Christendom today, the general idea is that it matters not what kind of religion one has, so long as he is sincere in what he believes. This is contrary to the Word of God. There are many religions — there may be many that are inviting to live by. But there is only ONE way to Heaven. Jesus said, "I am the way, I am the truth, I am the life. NO MAN COMETH UNTO THE FATHER BUT BY ME" (John 14:1-6). Jesus said, "I am the door"...not ONE of the doors...not A door — but "THE door." There is no back door nor side door to Heaven; there is only one door, and that door is Jesus.

There are many ways that look good and seem right — but they are each and every one the sidetracks of the devil and they lead to hell! If you or I hope to be in that happy number when the saints march into the Pearly White City, we must be saved by grace through faith in the shed blood of Jesus. When we put our trust in Jesus and believe on Him, God saves us "for Christ's sake" (Eph. 4:32).

In all three of the passages we have studied in this message, God had the *desire,* the people *decided against Him,* and God *destroyed* them.

In the first passage, God desired to bring Judah back unto Himself. He longed to forgive their sins and have them obedient to Him. But they said, "*We will not return!*" God had no alternative but to send disaster upon them.

In the second instance, Jesus looked out over Jerusalem and wept. He desired to protect His people — but they decided they wanted Barabbas instead of their Messiah. They asked for blood instead of accepting protection — therefore God destroyed them, declaring that their house was at that moment "desolate."

In our third Scripture, the king had the desire to have his friends and neighbors attend his son's wedding. He sent out the invitations, sent a second group to insist that they come — but they decided against it, went their separate ways, and the king sent his armies and destroyed them.

Nineteen hundred years ago, God desired to save the world and He sent His Son to die on the cross, "that whosoever believeth on Him might not perish, but have everlasting life." If we decide against Jesus and follow our own way, then God has no choice but to destroy us, and He will! Make no mistake — "The wages of sin is death; but the gift of God is eternal life through Jesus Christ our Lord." If you are not born again, dear friend, my advice to you is that you be saved right now. Today is the day of salvation. Now is the accepted time. If you put off salvation until tomorrow — even until the next hour — you may be destroyed. God desires to save you this moment — but if you decide against Jesus this moment you may be destroyed in the next moment. "Believe on the Lord Jesus Christ and thou shalt be saved" (Acts 16:31).

Chapter VI

Whosoever, Whatsoever, Not Whensoever

Whosoever, Whatsoever, Not Whensoever

"After this there was a feast of the Jews; and Jesus went up to Jerusalem. Now there is at Jerusalem by the sheep market a pool, which is called in the Hebrew tongue Bethesda, having five porches. In these lay a great multitude of impotent folk, of blind, halt, withered, waiting for the moving of the water. For an angel went down at a certain season into the pool, and troubled the water: whosoever then first after the troubling of the water stepped in was made whole of whatsoever disease he had.

"And a certain man was there, which had an infirmity thirty and eight years. When Jesus saw him lie, and knew that he had been now a long time in that case, He saith unto him, Wilt thou be made whole? The impotent man answered him, Sir, I have no man, when the water is troubled, to put me into the pool: but while I am coming, another steppeth down before me. Jesus saith unto him, Rise, take up thy bed, and walk. And immediately the man was made whole, and took up his bed, and walked: and on the same day was the Sabbath.

"The Jews therefore said unto him that was cured, It is the Sabbath day: it is not lawful for thee to carry thy bed. He answered them, He that made me whole, the same said unto me, Take up thy bed, and walk. Then asked they him, What man is that which said unto thee, Take up thy bed, and walk? And he that was healed wist not who it was: for Jesus had conveyed himself away, a multitude being in that place.

"Afterward Jesus findeth him in the temple, and said unto him, Behold, thou art made whole: sin no more, lest a worse thing come unto thee. The man departed, and told the Jews that it was Jesus, which had made him whole" (John 5:1-15).

Jesus had traveled to Jerusalem, the city of worship, to attend a feast of the Jews. He had just miraculously healed the nobleman's son (recorded in John 4:46-54). It was during the time of Christ's ministry on earth that the Jewish religion was the most popular of all religious faiths. Many thousands of Jews visited Jerusalem on feast days, where they purchased lambs and doves to offer as sacrifices for their sins.

The Scripture does not tell us what feast this was. It may have been the feast of Pentecost; but we do not know for sure. However, we do know that at such times, multitudes of worshippers passed through the sheep gate in the Jerusalem wall, and of necessity passed by the sheep market — only a stone's throw from the temple area.

In five porches around the pool, there lay a great multitude of impotent (sick) people. The Holy Spirit points out that some were blind, others were halt (lame), and still others were withered. They were waiting for the moving of the water. Each of the groups pointed out here symbolizes the sinner: *All sinners are blind.* If our gospel be hid, it is hid to them that are lost: in whom the God of this world hath blinded the minds of them which believe not (II Cor. 4:3-4). *All sinners are halt and withered.* (In the true sense, sinners are not only blind, halt, and withered — *they are dead.* Ephesians 2:1 tells us: "And you hath he quickened, who were dead in trespasses and sins.") Sinners are crippled — they cannot go where their God-given conscience tells them they *should* go. They cannot do what they know they *should* do. There are thousands of people who know, deep down in their heart, that they should live right, and they *desire* to live right — but in the flesh they find it impossible.

Thus we see that this miracle of the healing of the body went deeper than the physical. Jesus never healed any person simply for the sake of fleshly comfort. When Jesus healed someone physically, He was setting forth the truth that He had come to heal spiritually. When He said, "They that be whole need not a physician, but they that are sick" (Matt. 9:12), He was pointing to sickness of the soul by referring to sickness of the body.

In verse 4 of our present Scripture, we are told that at a certain season an angel went down into the pool and troubled the water. When this miraculous event occurred, *whosoever* first stepped into the pool was made whole of *whatsoever* disease he had.

WHOSOEVER

I believe in the sovereignty of God, but I cannot *explain* the sovereignty of God, nor do I understand it. I believe God knows the end in the beginning. God knows *who* will be saved, *when* they will be saved, and under what *conditions* they will be saved. But the *foreknowledge of God* has nothing to do with the *free will of man.*

Dear reader, forget what you have heard, or what you have been taught, and let us look together at the Word of God. "Let God be true, and every man a liar" (Rom. 3:4).

The text we are studying declares that WHOSOEVER first stepped in — was made whole. In that multitude of impotent folk, there must have been the rich and the poor, the white and the colored, the learned and the ignorant — but *whosoever* stepped in first, regardless of who he was, or from what social, monetary, or educational background he came, was made whole.

"For God so loved the world, He gave His only begotten Son, that whosoever believeth in Him should not perish, but have everlasting life" (John 3:16).

"And he is the propitiation for our sins: and not for ours only, but also for the sins of the whole world" (I John 2:2).

"But to as many as received him, to them gave he power to become the sons of God, even to them that believe on his name" (John 1:12).

While Jesus was here on earth, He had more trouble with His own people than with any other group. The Scribes and the Pharisees, the elders and the rulers in the temple, refused to hear Him and believe on Him. To this religious group, He said, "Search the Scriptures; for in them ye think ye have eternal life: and they are they which testify of me. And ye will not come to me, that ye might have life" (John 5:39-40).

Would Jesus have said, "Ye will not come to me, that ye might have life," if it were impossible for these people to come? Was Jesus speaking to a group who were not "elected"? It is true that He was speaking to a group who died in their sins and opened their eyes in hell; but the reason they were eternally lost was because they refused to come to Jesus, in whom is life.

Again Jesus said to His own people, "I said therefore unto you, that ye shall die in your sins: for if ye believe not that I am He, ye shall die in your sins" (John 8:24).

Why did Jesus say these people would die in their sins? Jesus clearly said, "Ye shall die in your sins, for *if ye believe not that I am He,* ye shall die in your sins!" Jesus declared that He was the Son of God, and had come to lay His life down for sinners — to take away the sins of the world. The miracles He performed declared Him to be more than man. On many occasions His listeners declared that He was from above. They said a man with a demon could not give sight to the blind, nor open the ears of the deaf. And yet, in spite of the miracles He performed before them day by day, many refused to believe. These were the ones who died in their sins and opened their eyes in hell, *because they refused to believe* that He was God's Son.

My dear friend, if you are so unfortunate as to spend eternity in the lake of fire, it will be because you refuse to receive the Lord Jesus Christ. The Bible clearly teaches, "He that believeth on Him is not condemned; but he that believeth not is condemned already, because he hath not believed in the name of the only begotten Son of God" (John 3:18).

I believe not only in the sovereignty of God, but also in the invisible body of Christ — the New Testament church. And I believe in the free will of man as taught in the Scriptures. Jesus said, "Come unto me, all ye that labor and are heavy laden, and I will give you rest" (Matt. 11:29). The invitation is, *"Come!"* Everybody is invited — YOU come! ANYone come! ALL come! *"Whosoever"* is thirsty, let him come and drink of the water of life freely.

Listen to these tender words: "The Lord is not slack concerning His promise, as some men count slackness; but is longsuffering to us-ward, not willing that any should perish, but that all should come to repentance" (II Peter 3:9). If I understand the language of the Holy Spirit, penned by the Apostle Peter, the Lord Jesus is not careless (slack) concerning the promise He has made: "He that cometh unto me, I will in no wise cast out" (John 6:37b). The Lord is faithful — He cannot lie. Therefore He is longsuffering to us-ward, to mankind. He is longsuffering because *He is not willing that any should perish.*

Does that mean what it says? Does it mean the Lord is not willing that ANY should perish? God did not create *one person* for hell — nor did He create hell for one person. (Hell was created for the devil.) It is not God's will that any person burn in hell; it is His will that all repent and receive the Lord Jesus Christ as their personal Saviour.

If you do not believe the Scriptures I have already given, I am sure you will not believe the one that follows. However, I must expose you to this passage — one of the most heart touching chapters in the Word of God. In the 53rd chapter of

Isaiah, the prophet declares, "He is despised and rejected of men; a man of sorrows, and acquainted with grief: and we hid as it were our faces from him; he was despised, and we esteemed him not. Surely he hath borne our griefs, and carried our sorrows: yet we did esteem him stricken, smitten of God, and afflicted. But he was wounded for our transgressions, he was bruised for our iniquities: the chastisement of our peace was upon him; and with his stripes we are healed" (Isa. 53:3-5). HERE IS THE CAPSTONE OF THE PYRAMID OF TRUTH: *WHOSOEVER WILL* CAN BE SAVED!

"ALL we like sheep have gone astray; we have turned every one to his own way; and the Lord [Jehovah] hath laid on him [Jesus] the iniquity of us all" (Isa. 53:6).

Insofar as I have been able to discover, this is the only verse in all the sixty-six books of the Bible that begins and ends with the same word. This verse tells me that *all men* have gone astray, there is none righteous — no, not one. We are altogether become unprofitable. We are ALL as an unclean thing. We are ALL sinners by nature — no one is excluded. But when Jehovah provided redemption, when Jehovah provided the sacrifice, He laid on the Lamb the iniquity of us all. I hasten to declare without reservation or hesitation that Jesus Christ paid the sin-debt for every sinner who has ever been born, or who ever *will* be born. His blood is sufficient to cover every sin that has ever been committed or ever will be committed — from Adam to the last person born on this earth. *"Whosoever"* can be saved if he will believe on the Lord Jesus Christ and receive Him by faith. Where you spend eternity, my friend, will depend upon whether or not you receive Jesus.

The sin-debt has been paid. Jesus, the Lamb of God, willingly laid His life down — once, for all, forever — never to be repeated. The blood of Jesus Christ, God's Son, cleanses from all sin. Salvation has been brought down, and is presented to *"whosoever will."* Your eternal destiny will be determined either by your willingness to accept the finished work of Jesus, or by your stubbornness in refusing to receive the gift of God—salvation by grace, through faith.

My dear friend, if you are not saved, and if you will face the fact that you are a sinner, you are included in the *"whosoever!"*

WHATSOEVER

Our text declares that whosoever first stepped into the pool was made whole of *whatsoever* disease he had. There were blind men there — withered men, men who were halt. I am sure that many other diseases were represented in that multitude of impotent folk who waited in the five porches around the pool. Our passage of Scripture records the story of Jesus healing the man who had been paralyzed for thirty-eight long years. *Whatsoever* his illness, *whosoever* stepped down first into the pool was healed.

There is a tremendous spiritual truth set forth here. Different drugs are used for treatment of different diseases today. Tuberculosis demands one treatment, whereas high blood pressure demands another. But in the spiritual aspect, the blood of Jesus Christ, God's Son, cleanses from *any and all sin.* There are no hard cases with Jesus. He can save the alcoholic just as easily and as quickly as He can save the seven-or eight-year-old boy or girl. Many times a physician is forced to leave a hospital room, shaking his head and declaring that he has done all he can do for the patient. But Jesus has never lost a case! Any sinner, regardless of how sinful he may be, can have his sins washed away in the blood of Jesus — the blood that cleanses from all unrighteousness. "Though your sins be as scarlet, they shall be as white as snow. Though they be red like crimson, they shall be as wool" (Isa. 1:18).

Let us examine briefly some of the converts of Jesus during His public ministry. John 3:1-21 tells of one of His first converts — Nicodemus. This man was a ruler of the Jews, a master in Israel, a ruler in the synagogue. He came to Jesus and addressed Him saying, "Rabbi, we know that thou art a teacher come from God: for no man can do these miracles that thou doest, except God be with him."

Jesus wasted no words in answering Nicodemus: "Verily, verily, I say unto thee, Except a man be born again, he cannot see the kingdom of God." Evidently Nicodemus showed some amazement or astonishment, for Jesus said, "*Marvel not* that I said unto thee, Ye must be born again." Nicodemus did not fully understand. He asked how an old man could be born. He marveled that Jesus would say to him — an educated, polished, religious man with a Master's degree — "Ye must be born again."

I believe Nicodemus was saved that day. If not, he certainly became a learner and was saved later, for he defended Jesus on one occasion a few days later. Then when Jesus was crucified, Nicodemus and Joseph of Arimathea claimed the body of their Lord and gave Him a proper burial. This convert was among the elite — he was religious, he was extraordinary in every sense of the word — but he was lost. He came to Jesus, he was saved, he was forgiven — he was born again.

In the conversion of Nicodemus lies one of the glorious truths of Redemption: that our Saviour can save from *whatsoever* — even from religion. There are thousands today who are religious but lost! It is often easier to reach the drunkard or the harlot with the message of salvation than it is to reach the person who is religious and lives a good, clean life. But Jesus saved Nicodemus from "*whatsover*," even from religion.

We will look next at a convert who was as despicable as Nicodemus was sublime. In John 4:1-29 Jesus departed into Galilee. In the course of His journey He visited Jacob's well, and while sitting on the well, He beheld a woman of Samaria come to draw water. He asked her for a drink, but she — knowing the

Jews and Samaritans hated each other — could not understand why Jesus should ask her, a Samaritan, for a drink.

Jesus told her He could give her *living* water. She thought He spoke of the water in the well; for she *asked* the Lord Jesus for a drink of this living water. Jesus then put her to the test — the test every sinner must face if he is seeking salvation — namely, are we willing to confess our sins to God? When Jesus asked the Samaritan woman to call her husband, she replied: "I have no husband!" Jesus commended her for telling the truth. He said, "For thou hast had five husbands, and he whom thou now hast is NOT thine husband. In that, saidst thou truly!"

When Jesus told the woman exactly how many husbands she had had and that the person she was now living with was not her husband, she knew that she was in the presence of more than a man. Every sinner must recognize that Jesus is more than man — that He is the Son of God — if he wants salvation. We must confess that Jesus died for our sins according to the Scriptures, that He was buried, and that He rose again the third day according to the Scriptures. The person who recognizes these Bible facts and puts his faith in the Christ who came, suffered, died, was buried, and rose again, will be saved by God's grace.

After the woman said, "I perceive that thou art a prophet," she began to talk to Jesus about a place to worship. But she was not ready to worship. Because Jesus knew the devil was trying to sidetrack her and get her mind on the *place* to worship, instead of the *one* whom she should worship, He said, "Ye worship ye know not what. We know what we worship . . . for salvation is of the Jews."

The woman had heard the story of the coming of Jesus — perhaps from a godly mother, perhaps from a godly grandmother. She said, "I know that Messiah cometh, which is called Christ. And when he is come, he will tell us all things." It was when

Jesus heard her make this confession that He knew the woman was ready for salvation.

It is only when a person believes with all of his heart that Jesus is the Christ, the Son of God — omnipotent, omniscient, and omnipresent — that he is ready for salvation. Jesus said to the woman: "I THAT SPEAK UNTO THEE AM HE!" (John 4:26). He spoke only seven words — but the woman *believed* these seven words and was gloriously saved! She threw down her waterpots and ran to town, where she told the men that she had met a man who told her everything she had ever done. She confessed to the men, "This is the Christ!" Then the men went out to see Jesus, and a revival broke out. Thus, the homewrecking, heartbreaking harlot became a soul-winning woman.

Yes, Jesus saved Dr. Nicodemus, the outstanding religionist. He saved the woman of Samaria, a heartbreaking harlot. And in John 4:46-54 we read of where He saved the entire household of an outstanding nobleman. From that home, Jesus went to Jerusalem at feast time. It was at the pool of Bethesda that He saved and healed a precious man who had been paralyzed for thirty-eight years.

Regardless of *who you* are or *what* you are, Jesus can and will save you. I wonder if I am speaking to some alcoholic? Perhaps I am speaking to a doper, or an habitual gambler. Perhaps I am speaking to some person who is guilty of a sin too horrible to mention, too ugly to talk about. Perhaps you have drunk deeply of the bitter dregs of the cup of sin. Perhaps you have stooped so low, gone so far, that your own mother has turned her back on you. But dear friend, when mother and father forsake you, when friends and loved ones do not want you in their company, when you become so dirty, vile, sinful, and ungodly that the jailer does not even want you in his jail, Jesus will gladly receive you if you will only believe on Him and trust Him as your personal Saviour.

Listen to Jesus in His dying hour: "Father, forgive them; for they know not what they do" (Luke 23:34). While Jesus hung on the cross, the two thieves railed on Him and mocked Him. They sneered and jeered; but after awhile, one of the thieves — seeing something in His face, or hearing something in the words He spoke — changed his mind about Him. Just before Jesus died, this thief looked over at the middle cross and said, "Lord, remember me when thou comest into thy kingdom!" In response to those pleading words, Jesus said, "Verily, I say unto thee, today shalt thou be with me in paradise" (Luke 23:42-43). That thief was saved during the last moments of our Lord's earthly life.

God help me to drive home to your precious heart, dear reader, that if you are not saved, never let the devil or any preacher tell you that you are too great a sinner to be saved, that you are too wicked to be saved. God will forgive you of "WHATSOEVER" sin you may have committed. The sin that will damn your soul and condemn you to the lake of fire will be the sin of rejecting the Lord Jesus Christ. "He that believeth not is condemned already, BECAUSE HE HATH NOT BELIEVED IN THE NAME OF THE ONLY BEGOTTEN SON OF GOD" (John 3:18b).

The Publican prayed, "God, be merciful to me, a sinner," and he went home justified (saved) (Luke 18:13). If you, dear reader, are not born again, bow your head, and in your own words, in your own way, simply ask the Lord Jesus to come into your heart, forgive your sins, and save you. He will do it! Pray to Him from your heart, and He will save you from *"whatsoever!"*

NOT WHENSOEVER

The Scriptures make it plain that *whosoever* can be saved from *whatsoever* sin — but NOT WHENSOEVER. Sinner friend, you cannot burn the candle of life for the devil and serve him until you make up your mind that you have had enough of sin. You cannot use God's grace as a fire insurance policy, nor can you acquire salvation as you would take an insurance policy on your home or your automobile.

God loves the whole world; Jesus died for all sinners; ALL are invited to come — NOW! "NOW is the accepted time, behold, TODAY is the day of salvation!" (II Cor. 6:2). Dear unbeliever, if you will bow your head this very moment and call upon the name of the Lord, I guarantee you on the basis of His Word, *He will save you.* But if you put it off until five minutes from now, you may wait too long. NOW, as you read these words, NOW is the accepted time.

You have heard it said that "as long as there is life, there is hope." But is that true? As long as there is life, is there really hope? Suppose we let the Word of God answer that question: "Because I have called, and ye have refused; I have stretched out my hand, and no man regarded; but ye have set at nought all my counsel, and would none of my reproof: I ALSO WILL LAUGH AT YOUR CALAMITY; I WILL MOCK WHEN YOUR FEAR COMETH; When our fear cometh as desolation, and our destruction cometh as a whirlwind; when distress and anguish cometh upon you. Then shall they call upon me, but I will not answer; they shall seek me early, but they shall not find me: FOR THAT THEY HATED KNOWLEDGE, AND DID NOT CHOOSE THE FEAR OF THE LORD" (Prov. 1:24-29).

Please notice: *They hated knowledge. They did not choose the fear of the Lord.* It clearly declares: "They hated knowledge." Proverbs 1:7 clearly defines *knowledge:* "The fear of the Lord is the beginning of knowledge." They did not choose the fear of the Lord.

"They would none of my counsel: they despised all my reproof. Therefore shall they eat of the fruit of their own way, and be filled with their own devices" (Prov. 1:30-31).

I beg you to hear the solemn warning of these verses, penned by the man of wisdom under inspiration of God. "I called — you refused. I stretched out my hand — you would not regard it. You set at naught my counsel. You would not listen to my reproof. Therefore, *I will laugh at your calamity!* And when your fear comes as a tornado, I will not answer. You will seek me, but you will not find me!" That is God's holy Word; to reject it does not change its warnings.

Hear the words of Isaiah: "Seek ye the Lord while He may be found; call ye upon Him while He is near" (Isa. 55:6). Does that not suggest to you that there may be a time when you will seek the Lord and can not find Him? If there could be no such time, why does Isaiah warn us to seek the Lord while He may be found, to call upon Him while He is near?

Hear the words of the Apostle Paul: "Because that, when they knew God, they glorified him not as God, neither were thankful; but became vain in their imaginations, and their foolish heart was darkened. Professing themselves to be wise, they became fools, and changed the glory of the uncorruptible God into an image made like to corruptible man, and to birds, and four-footed beasts, and creeping things. Wherefore GOD ALSO GAVE THEM UP TO UNCLEANNESS THROUGH THE LUSTS OF THEIR OWN HEARTS, TO DISHONOUR THEIR OWN BODIES BETWEEN THEMSELVES" (Rom. 1:21-24).

Paul is describing a group of people who knew God — but they refused to *glorify* God. They were unthankful; they professed to be wise; they changed the glory of the uncorruptible God into an image — an idol — *and God gave them up!*

"Who changed the truth of God into a lie, and worshipped and served the creature more than the Creator, who is blessed for ever. Amen. For this cause God gave them up unto vile affections: for even their women did change the natural use into that which is against nature" (Rom. 1:25-26). In these verses Paul describes a group who changed God's Word into a lie. They said, in effect, that God did not mean what He said, one does not need to be born again, there is no everlasting hell — and if there were an everlasting hell God would not permit any person to go there! These people changed God's truth to read in a way that sounds good to the unregenerate — they changed God's truth into a lie, *and God gave them up!*

"And even as they did not like to retain God in their knowledge, God gave them over to a reprobate mind, to do those things which are not convenient" (Rom. 1:28). Here is a group who did not like to retain God in their knowledge. They did not like to think about God, or the things of God. They had pleasure in unrighteousness — fornication, wickedness, covetousness, maliciousness, envy — and *God gave them up* to a reprobate (corrupt, depraved) mind!

We have just read the descriptions of three groups of people who were given up by Almighty God. I believe there are people today who are just as sure to burn in hell as the sun is sure to rise in the morning because they know about God and yet refuse to glorify Him *as* God. They do not believe the truth of God, they make the Bible say *what they want it to say.* (They can enjoy a double feature at the movies, or a bullfight in Mexico — but if the minister preaches more than fifteen minutes on Sunday morning, they become furious!) They do not like to retain God in their thinking. In Hosea 4:17 God said, "Ephraim is joined to idols: let him alone..." and when GOD says, "Let him alone," that person is sure to burn in the lake of fire.

John 6:44 gives another solemn warning concerning the NOW of salvation: "NO MAN CAN COME TO ME, EXCEPT THE FATHER WHICH HATH SENT ME DRAW HIM: AND I WILL RAISE HIM UP AT THE LAST DAY." That settles it! No person can come to Jesus for salvation except the Heavenly Father draw him. But how does God draw the sinner?

The answer is clearly given in the Word of God: "For whosoever shall call upon the name of the Lord shall be saved. How then shall they call on him in whom they have not believed? and how shall they believe on him of whom they have not heard? and how shall they hear without a preacher? and how shall they preach except they be sent? as it is written, How beautiful are the feet of them that preach the gospel of peace and bring glad tidings of good things!...so then, faith cometh by hearing, and hearing by the word of God" (Rom. 10:13-17).

Here is God's plan of salvation: *Whosoever shall call* — that takes in everyone, it excludes no one — WHOSOEVER! *They cannot call until they believe*. They cannot believe *until they hear the Word of God*. They *cannot hear without a preacher* — and the preacher cannot preach *except he be sent*.

God calls and sends out preachers. God's preachers preach the Word. "Faith cometh by hearing, and hearing by the Word of God." The unbeliever hears the Word and believes the Word. Believing the Word brings faith to the heart; and faith exercised in the Christ who IS the Word, brings saving grace. When the unbeliever believes that Jesus is the Christ and that He died to save sinners, he will call upon the name of the Lord; and "Whosoever shall call upon the name of the Lord shall be saved!"

My precious unbeliever, do not put off salvation another moment. Receive the Lord Jesus Christ and be saved. He left the Father's bosom, He left Heaven's glory, He left the angels, and came to this world — not to be ministered unto, but to minister, and to give His life a ransom for many.

Volumes have been written about Jesus — yet Luke sums up His mission to this earth in one short verse: "For the Son of man is come to seek and to save that which was lost" (Luke 19:10). As you read these lines, dear unbeliever, Jesus is seeking you through the gospel — through the Word of God that I have given in this message. You are among the *whosoever*. God can and will save you from *whatsoever* sins you have committed. But *not whensoever!* You must do it now. God has called, He has stretched out His hand, He has invited you — and if you set at naught His counsel, if you refuse His outstretched hand, you may never have another chance to be saved!

Today is the day of salvation. NOW is the accepted time. If you are not saved, please bow your head right where you are — and call upon the name of the Lord. "Believe on the Lord Jesus Christ, and thou shalt be saved" (Acts 16:31).

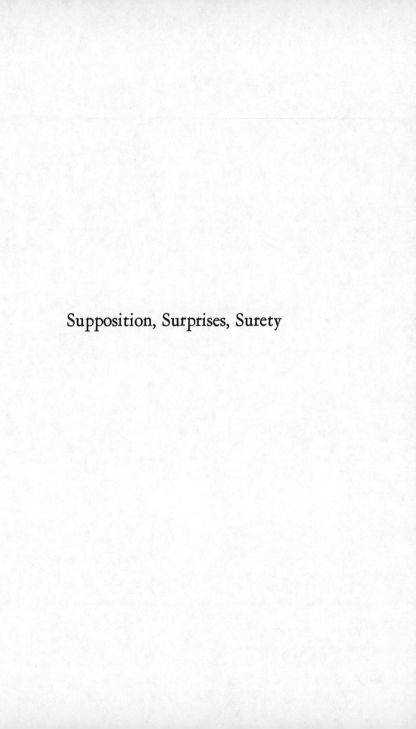

Supposition, Surprises, Surety

Information Systems Security

Chapter VII

Supposition, Surprises, Surety

"Now his parents went to Jerusalem every year at the feast of the passover. And when he was twelve years old, they went up to Jerusalem after the custom of the feast. And when they had fulfilled the days, as they returned, the child Jesus tarried behind in Jerusalem; and Joseph and his mother knew not of it. But they, *supposing* him to have been in the company, went a day's journey; and they sought him among their kinsfolk and acquaintance. And when they found him not, they turned back again to Jerusalem, seeking him.

"And it came to pass, that *after three days* they found him in the temple, sitting in the midst of the doctors, both hearing them, and asking them questions. And all that heard him were astonished at his understanding and answers.

"And when they saw him, they were amazed: and his mother said unto him, Son, why hast thou thus dealt with us? Behold, thy father and I have sought thee sorrowing. And he said unto them, How is it that ye sought me? Wist ye not that I must be about my Father's business?" (Luke 2:41-49).

SUPPOSITION AND THE BELIEVER

In this message I want us to study *supposition, surprises,* and *surety,* as having to do with both the believer and the UNbeliever.

Note verse 44: "But they, *supposing* him to have been in the company, went a day's journey; and they sought him among their kinsfolk and acquaintance."

These verses deal with Jesus and His parents at the first Passover He attended. At the age of twelve He was taken by Mary His mother and Joseph to the temple in Jerusalem to attend the Passover; when the ceremonies were over, they departed from Jerusalem, but neglected to make sure that Jesus was with them. (They *supposed* Him to have been in the company.)

The dictionary defines *suppose* as *An opinion entertained without positive knowledge, or without special thought of error.* Mary and Joseph supposed that Jesus was with them — but they did not know for sure — they did not consider the possibility of error.

We should never "suppose" when dealing with spiritual matters. We should be certain that we have actually met the Lord Jesus Christ in genuine repentance and faith. God forbid that any person who claims to be a Christian should be living on supposition. Let me illustrate. If I should ask whether or not you are an American citizen, you would immediately answer without hesitancy, "Yes," if you *were* an American citizen. Proud to be an American citizen, you would not just say, "Well, I *suppose* I am an American." Yet many times when I ask a person, "Are you a *Christian?*" he answers: "Well, I *suppose* I am... I am a church member." Or, "I *suppose* I am... I have been baptized." "I *suppose* I am... I have been attending church since I was a child."

Beloved, that is not the clear-cut testimony of a born-again believer. *We know* that we have passed from death unto life; *we know* our names are written in the Lamb's book of life. How do we know? "For the Spirit himself beareth witness with our spirit, that we are the children of God" (Rom. 8:16). "We know that we have passed from death unto life, because we love the brethren (I John 3:14). There is no such thing as a salvation based on supposition. If we just *suppose* we have met God, it is evident that we have NOT met Him. When we are born again, Jesus abides in us in the Person of the Holy Spirit. God lives in us! According to Romans 8:9 no person is saved who does not possess the Holy Spirit. Do you "suppose" that Jesus is in your heart? Or do you KNOW FOR SURE that He abides within?

There is a deep spiritual message here for the believer. Mary, the mother of Jesus, knew He was the Son of God. Joseph also knew who He was, because God had appeared to him in a dream and assured him that Jesus was conceived of the Holy Ghost. Therefore, even though in our present Scripture they had lost His presence and were not enjoying the warmth of His smile, the tenderness of His words, *He was still their child.* They lost communion and fellowship with Him — but His relationship to them remained the same. They were so occupied with the things around them that they did not miss the presence of Jesus for an entire day! It is alarming and astounding to think that the virgin whom God honored as no other woman has ever been honored, would permit miles to separate her from the presence of Jesus, while she just "supposed" that so precious a Jewel was in the company! It seems she would have made sure.

Beloved, I think God permitted this to happen that you and I might understand a little more fully how finite we are, how careless we can be, and how totally dependent we are upon Him.

Perhaps Mary and Joseph were talking with friends and relatives whom they had not seen for a long time. I am sure they were occupied every moment of that day as they walked the dusty road; but nowhere in the record are we told that even once during the entire day did Mary and Joseph ask each other, "Where is the child Jesus?" They lived *one day* of supposition, and it cost them *three days* of heartbreak and sorrow as they searched for the child. They searched among their kinsmen, among their acquaintances; they looked everywhere; and after backtracking for three days over the same distance they had traveled in *one* day without Him, they found Him in the exact spot where they had left Him! They found Him in the temple, sitting in the midst of the doctors, hearing them and asking them questions — astounding them with His wisdom and understanding.

Beloved, this was the same crowd who finally crucified Jesus. Had they known who He was that day, they would no doubt have attempted to put Him to death. But God kept His Son's identity hidden. Jesus came to pay sin's debt on the cross. In spite of the carelessness of His mother and Joseph, God the Father took care of His only begotten Son and saw Him through to the old rugged cross, according to divine plan.

The Bible admonition to the believer is this: "But sanctify the Lord God in your hearts: and be ready always to give an answer to every man that asketh you a reason of the hope that is in you with meekness and fear" (I Peter 3:15).

Have a definite, positive experience that gives assurance, that makes it possible for you to give an answer to anyone who asks you concerning the hope you have in God, and your life in Christ.

Peter says, "Wherefore the rather, brethren, give diligence to make your calling and election sure: for if ye do these things, ye shall never fall" (II Peter 1:10). What Peter is saying to us here is simply this: "Leave no stone unturned — go to all limits — exhaust every avenue in *making sure* and positively *knowing* that you are prepared to meet God."

Is such assurance possible? I answer in the words of Holy Scripture: "... I KNOW WHOM I HAVE BELIEVED, and am persuaded that he is able to keep that which I have committed unto him against that day" (II Tim. 1:12b). Yes, *we can know*. Paul did not "suppose." He had a positive, "know-so" salvation. If you do not know that you are born again, that the Holy Spirit abides in your heart, it is evident that He is not there. God is no respecter of persons. If God gave Paul a "know-so" salvation, He will give you and me the same positive assurance of *our* salvation.

Believers are not to trust in supposition. We are to "have faith in God" (Mark 11:22). We *know* whom we have believed. We *know* we have passed from death unto life, because the Holy Spirit witnesses within the inner man. We do not *suppose* concerning right and wrong; we prove all things, we hold fast that which is good. We do not *suppose* that a thing will be all right—then go ahead and do it. If we pray, seeking God's will, He will lead us into paths of righteousness for His name's sake. Believers live by *faith* — not by supposition: "*The just shall live by faith.*"

Mark 6:45-52 records another case of supposition on the part of believers: "And straightway he constrained his disciples to get into the ship, and to go to the other side before Bethsaida, while he sent away the people. And when he had sent them away, he departed into a mountain to pray. And when even was come, the ship was in the midst of the sea, and he alone on the land. And he saw them toiling in rowing; for the wind was contrary unto them: and about the fourth watch of the night he cometh unto them, walking upon the sea, and would have passed by them. But when they saw him walking upon the sea, they *supposed* it had been a spirit, and cried out: For they all saw him, and were troubled. And immediately he talked with them, and saith unto them, Be of good cheer: it is I; be not afraid."

Note verse 49: "But when they saw him walking upon the sea, they SUPPOSED it had been a spirit, and cried out..." Jesus had just fed five thousand people and had sent the disciples across the sea of Galilee in a little boat. The sea of Galilee is noted for storms that can arise in a matter of minutes.

Such a storm arose when the disciples were in the middle

of the sea. Toiling at the oars, the wind blowing contrary to them, they thought their boat was going to sink. Jesus seeing them understood the predicament they were in — and started walking to them on the water. Have you ever been out on a lake, rowing or fishing, and had someone come to you *walking on the water?* If not, do not be too hard on Peter and those who were with him. Put yourself in their place and ask yourself, "What would *I* have done had I been in that little ship that night?"

It seems to you and me that when the disciples saw Jesus walking upon the sea, they would have recognized Him with whom they had been just a few hours before; but they did not recognize Him. What was happening was so unusual that they could not comprehend it. They *supposed* they were looking at a spirit — they thought they were *"seeing a ghost"* — and it frightened them. Mark tells us Jesus would have passed on by — but they called out to Him. He would have passed them by had they not invited His company.

The same story is given in Matthew 14:22-23. Jesus said, "It is I. Be not afraid," and Peter said, "Lord if it be thou, bid me come unto thee on the water." As long as Peter kept his eyes on Jesus he walked on the water; but when he looked at the boisterous waves around his feet he began to sink. When he cried "Lord, save me!" the Lord reached down and lifted him up.

Jesus wants to abide with you when all is well; but He also wants to abide with you when the storm clouds hang low, when the contrary winds are blowing and when the waves beat all around you. He wants to abide in every secret chamber of your life — but He will never force Himself upon anyone. If you do not give Him an invitation, He will pass on by.

In Luke 24:13-35 we find the account of the disciples walking to Emmaus the day Jesus rose from the dead. As the two disciples walked along the dusty road, talking sadly of the things that had happened in Jerusalem in the previous three days, a Stranger joined them and conversed with them. The Scriptures tell us that when they reached Emmaus, "They drew nigh unto the village, whither they went: AND HE MADE AS THOUGH HE WOULD HAVE GONE FURTHER. But they constrained Him, saying, Abide with us: for it is toward evening, and the day is far spent. And He went in to tarry with them."

Great blessing followed. As He broke bread, they saw the scars in His hands and they recognized Him. Then they confessed, "Did not our heart burn within us, while he talked with us by the way, and while he opened to us the Scriptures?" Yes, Jesus will abide, He *wants* to abide, He does abide with the disciples who make Him welcome. If we will extend to Him an invitation, He will give to us His abiding presence and an abundance of His grace.

Supposition could have caused the little ship to sink. Supposition could have robbed the disciples of rich blessing on the road to Emmaus, had they permitted the Stranger to continue on His journey. But they constrained Him, He went in with them — and blessing followed.

SUPPOSITION AND THE SINNER

"And from thence to Philippi, which is the chief city of that part of Macedonia, and a colony: and we were in that city abiding certain days. And on the Sabbath we went out of the city by a river side, where prayer was wont to be made; and we sat down, and spake unto the women which resorted thither. And a certain woman named Lydia, a seller of purple, of the city of Thyatira, which worshipped God, heard us: whose heart the Lord opened, and she attended unto the things which were spoken of Paul. And when she was baptized, and her household, she besought us, saying, If ye have judged me to be faithful to the Lord, come into my house, and abide there. And she constrained us.

"And it came to pass, as we went to prayer, a certain damsel possessed with a spirit of divination met us, which brought her masters much gain by soothsaying: The same followed Paul and us, and cried, saying, These men are the servants of the most high God, which show unto us the way of salvation. And this she did many days. But Paul, being grieved, turned and said to the spirit, I command thee in the name of Jesus Christ to come out of her. And he came out the same hour. And when her masters saw that the hope of their gains was gone, they caught Paul and Silas, and drew them into the marketplace unto the rulers, and brought them to the magistrates, saying, These men, being Jews, do exceedingly trouble our city, and teach customs, which are not lawful for us to receive, neither to observe, being Romans. And the multitude rose up together against them: and the magistrates rent off their clothes, and commanded to beat them. And when they had laid many stripes upon them, they cast them into prison, charging the jailor to keep them safely: Who, having received such a charge, thrust them into the inner prison, and made their feet fast in the stocks.

"And at midnight Paul and Silas prayed, and sang praises unto God: and the prisoners heard them. And suddenly there was a great earthquake, so that the foundations of the prison were shaken: and immediately all the doors were opened, and every one's bands were loosed. And the keeper of the prison awaking out of his sleep, and seeing the prison doors open, he drew out his sword, and would have killed himself, supposing that the prisoners had been fled. But Paul cried with a loud voice, saying, Do thyself no harm: for we are all here. Then he called for a light, and sprang in, and came trembling, and fell down before Paul and Silas, and brought them out, and said, Sirs, what must I do to be saved? And they said, Believe on the Lord Jesus Christ, and thou shalt be saved, and thy house. And they spake unto him the word of the Lord, and to all that were in his house. And he took them the same hour of the night, and washed their stripes; and was baptized, he and all his, straightway. And when he had brought them into his house, he set meat before them, and rejoiced, believing in God with all his house" (Acts 16:12-34).

In this passage we have the account of three marvelous conversions. Lydia, the first convert in Europe under the ministry of the Apostle Paul, was a lady of the elite. A merchant in Thyatira, she dealt in purple and fine linen — worn in that day only by the wealthy. Lydia was an outstanding lady of the city of Thyatira. She worshipped God, but she had not experienced the grace of God. She was the leader of a prayer band, and when Paul spoke to the group, she was converted. She was then baptized and constrained Paul to spend some time in her home.

The second convert in this Scripture was quite the opposite of Lydia. She was a fortune teller who followed Paul and Silas for several days. She heard the message of Paul over and over again. Herein lies a tremendous truth. It was perhaps the first gospel this poor woman had ever heard; yet as she listened day by day, her heart softened and she cried out, "These men are the servants of the most high God, which show us the way of salvation!"

As Paul preached the message of salvation and this soothsayer listened, she was saved. The men who made their living through the work of this woman became very angry when she gave up fortunetelling. They had Paul and Silas beaten and thrown in prison, charging the jailor to be very sure they did not escape. To insure their safe keeping he put them in the inner prison in the dungeon, and made their feet fast in the stocks.

God's man may be locked in a dungeon — but God cannot be locked out! At midnight Paul and Silas prayed. They probably had no supper that night; they were bleeding from the severe beatings they had endured; they were in much pain; but under these adverse circumstances they *sang, praised God* — and *prayed!*

Suddenly, there was an earthquake — (I think God must have said "Amen!"). The whole earth shook and trembled. The prison doors were opened, all the shackles and bonds were loosed. This great commotion awakened the keeper of the prison from his sleep. The first thing he saw was that all the doors were open, all the chains were loosed, and the prisoners were free. He drew out his sword — "and would have killed himself, SUPPOSING that the prisoners had been fled!"

The jailer was about to take his own life, supposing that the prisoners had escaped. In his day, under his government, he knew he would pay for their escape with his own life. Had he taken his life, he would also have taken a short cut to hell — for he was an unbeliever. Always looking for an opportunity to point someone to Jesus, Paul cried out, *"Do thyself no harm! We are all here!"*

The jailer must have been astonished beyond measure that prisoners who could have escaped did not run! He was trembling. He called for a light, came in, and fell on his knees, saying to Paul and Silas, "Sirs, WHAT MUST I DO TO BE SAVED?" Paul and Silas immediately told him, "BELIEVE ON THE LORD JESUS CHRIST, AND THOU SHALT BE SAVED, AND THY HOUSE!"

Paul and Silas then went to the jailer's home, where they "spake unto him the word of the Lord, and to all that were in his house." They taught the way of salvation by grace through faith to those in the jailer's house. And as Paul and Silas spoke the Word of God to the jailer and to all that were in his house, the Word brought faith, the lost ones exercised faith — and God saved them!

Afterwards, the jailer washed the backs of Paul and Silas and dressed their wounds. Then he and all of his household were baptized. After the baptism, he set meat before them — AND RE-

JOICED, BELIEVING IN GOD WITH ALL HIS HOUSE.

Thank God, the jailer's supposition which almost sent him to hell, became a miracle that brought salvation through the teaching of the Word of God when Paul and Silas sat in the jailer's house and instructed his entire household in the way of life.

Dear reader, have YOU said, "Salvation is all right for others — but I do not suppose it is for ME! Salvation is all right for some people, but I do not suppose I was included!" *Do not go to hell on a supposition!* Hear the word of the Lord! "God so loved the world . . ." and you are part of the world that He loved. God gave Jesus to die on the cross, that "whosoever [YOU are among the whosoever] believeth on him should not perish, but have everlasting life." "Believe on the Lord Jesus Christ and thou shalt be saved." Do it this very moment!

Another tremendous passage that sets forth the truth I have just given is found in Acts 27. Read the entire chapter. Paul being sent by ship to Rome, came to a place called The Fair Havens — a place where the ships dropped anchor and waited out the winter storms. The storm season being only a few days away, the captain of the ship took a vote, and the sailors voted to sail on; but Paul admonished them saying, "Sirs, I perceive that this voyage will be with hurt and much damage, not only of the lading and ship, but also of our lives. Nevertheless, the centurion believed the master and the owner of the ship, more than those things which were spoken by Paul. And because The Haven was not commodious to winter in, the more part advised to depart thence also, if by any means they might attain to Phenice, and there to winter; which is an haven of Crete, and lieth toward the south west and north west. And when the south wind blew softly, SUPPOSING *that they had obtained their purpose,* loosing thence, they sailed close by Crete" (Acts 27:10-13).

Here is the picture: God's preacher said to the captain of the ship, "Do not leave the Fair Havens." But the sailors said, "We want to go to Phenice where there are lights and dance halls and taverns. Fair Havens is not commodious — not inviting or roomy. There are no bright lights." Paying no attention to Paul, they sailed. For several days the south wind blew. They *supposed* they had done the right thing, but when they were right out in the middle of the sea the storm broke about them, caught the ship, and drove it mercilessly. The ship tossed, tumbled, and rolled — for many days they saw neither sun nor stars. The storm grew worse and worse, until "all hope that we should be saved was taken away" (Acts 27:20). At this point, Paul went down into the hull of the ship and *prayed*. God answered him, and when Paul came back up on deck he said to the men, "I exhort you to be of good cheer!" He told them that God had sent His angel to assure him that all lives would be saved, even though the ship would be lost. "Wherefore sirs, be of good cheer: FOR I BELIEVE GOD, that it shall be even as it was told me" (Acts 27:25). The remainder of the chapter tells us that the ship was completely destroyed, but all lives were saved — ONLY BECAUSE of God's man who delivered the message of truth at the beginning of the voyage — the message that was rejected and ignored. The men *supposed* they knew more than did a fanatical preacher, and they sailed against his warning. Yet when death would have swallowed them up, God had mercy on the passengers and saved the life of every one, through the prayers of one believer!

Dear reader, when God's preacher preaches God's Word, do not take issue with what he has to say. Do not *SUPPOSE* you know better than he. Do not SUPPOSE you are right and he is wrong. When God's preacher delivers God's message and declares, "Thus saith the Lord," accept it as God's truth. Do not *suppose anything* having to do with your eternal destiny. You may well end up in the hurricanes of hell and thus be eternally destroyed in the lake of fire and brimstone!

SURPRISES THAT AWAIT THEM WHO BELIEVE

The Scriptures give some very interesting accounts of men and women with "religion" who met with great surprises.

NICODEMUS. Nicodemus was the epitome of honesty, integrity, and religious background. He was a Pharisee of the Pharisees, a ruler of the Jews, a master in Israel. Clean, upright, and sincere, he went to Jesus with a sincere heart, and said to Him: "Rabbi, we know that thou art a teacher come from God: for no man can do these miracles that thou doest, except God be with him" (John 3:2). Poor Nicodemus was a religious sinner. He was sincere — but he was sincerely lost, as are a lot of people today.

Jesus answered Nicodemus in clear, understandable words: "Verily, verily, I say unto thee, Except a man be born again he cannot see the kingdom of God" (John 3:3). Nicodemus asked out of a sincere heart: "How can an old man be born? Can he enter the second time into his mother's womb, and be born?"

Jesus instructed him that He was not speaking of a fleshly birth, but of a spiritual birth.... "That which is born of the flesh is flesh, and that which is born of the Spirit is spirit" (John 3:6). When Jesus spoke those words of conviction and life, Nicodemus undoubtedly displayed surprise and astonishment, because Jesus looked at him and said, *"Marvel not* that I said unto thee, Ye must be born again" (John 3:7). The dictionary defines *marvel* as: "to excite wonder; surprising; extraordinary; sometimes strange and surprising to the point of being improbable or incredible." The fact that Jesus said *"Marvel not"* suggests that Nicodemus was surprised that this Great Teacher told *him* — a man who was clean, religious, upright, a ruler of the Jews, a master in Israel — that he must be completely made over — *reborn.*

Jesus then gave him the illustration of Moses and the brazen serpent in the wilderness. Since Nicodemus was a master in Israel, he knew what the brass stood for. He knew about the pole and the serpent. I believe Nicodemus was saved that day — at least he was convinced that he needed a Saviour, and finally accepted the salvation that only the new birth can bring to the human heart. I believe Nicodemus was surprised beyond measure when the Greatest of all Teachers instructed him that it was absolutely imperative that *he, Dr. Nicodemus,* be born again before he could enter the kingdom of Heaven.

THE SAMARITAN WOMAN. Read John 4:1-39. In these verses we find Jesus had departed into Galilee, and He "must needs go through Samaria." Stopping at Jacob's well, He sat resting, when a woman of Samaria — an exceedingly sinful woman — came to the well. Before she had time to speak, Jesus asked her for a drink. This was a great surprise to her. The hatred between the Jews and Samaritans was as deep as any racial hatred has ever been. Bible history tells us that the Jews prayed each morning that God would deliver them from seeing the face of a Samaritan that day.

Her surprise caused her to ask, "HOW IS IT THAT THOU, BEING A JEW, ASKEST DRINK OF ME, WHICH AM A WOMAN OF SAMARIA? For the Jews have no dealings with the Samaritans!" She was surprised and astonished beyond measure. In effect, she said, "I simply do not understand it!"

In the course of the conversation, Jesus said, "If you knew who I am, you would ask me for a drink — and I would give you living water." The woman answered, "The well is deep, and you have nothing with which to draw. How can you give me this living water?" Jesus replied, "The water you drink from this well does not quench your thirst... you must drink again; but the water I can give you will be in you a well of water, springing up into everlasting life." When Jesus made that statement, the woman said, "Give me this water!" Jesus then said, "Go call thy husband," and she immediately answered, "I have no husband." Jesus said, "You have told the truth. You have no husband.... you have had five husbands, and he whom you now have is not your husband."

At this point, the woman displayed her knowledge of religion and the Bible. She said, "The Jews say Jerusalem is the place to worship; but my fathers worshipped in this mountain. I know Messiah is coming, and when he comes he will tell us all things." But this woman was not ready to worship — in Jerusalem, in the mountain, or anywhere else. She needed to meet the Messiah. So Jesus said, "I that speak unto thee am HE" (John 4:26). When Jesus said that, she threw down her waterpots and ran to town. She told the townsmen she had met a man who told her everything she ever did — and she said, "Is not this the Christ? Men, I have found the Messiah! And He gave me living water!" *And the heartbreaking harlot became a soul-winning evangelist, who turned the whole neighborhood to Jesus!*

Yes, she was surprised when a Jew asked her, a hated Samaritan, for a drink; but her surprise led to her salvation! Is there not a lesson here for preachers of the gospel today? When we go into the pulpit and preach the straight gospel of Truth, it will surprise some people. But they need to be surprised — they need salvation!

THE WOMAN TAKEN IN ADULTERY. In John 8:1-11 we have the account of another group who were surprised beyond measure. Having been to the Mount of Olives, Jesus was in the temple teaching the morning Bible class. The Word tells us, "And all the people came unto him; and he sat down, and taught them" (John 8:2). Jesus sat in the midst of them, teaching them, when suddenly the religious leaders of the community came rushing in. The Scripture says "...The Scribes and Pharisees brought unto him a woman taken in adultery; and they sat her in the midst."

That was something to behold. A group of men bringing a woman into the assembly and setting her down in the midst of the people. The spokesman for the group said, "Master, this woman was taken in adultery, in the very act. Now Moses in the Law commanded us that such should be stoned...but what sayest thou?" (John 8:4-5). These religious leaders were not interested in the salvation of the poor adulteress; *they were tempting the Lord Jesus.*

This group of religionists were forever searching for something through which to accuse the Lord Jesus; but I am sure they were surprised beyond measure when the Son of God answered not a word. "Jesus stooped down, and with his finger wrote on the ground, as though he heard them not." They kept on asking Jesus, and He "lifted up himself, and said unto them, he that is without sin among you, let him first cast a stone at her. And again he stooped down, and wrote on the ground."

I do not know what He wrote — but whatever it was it not only surprised them — it convicted them as well; and one by one they walked away! Jesus and the woman were left alone in the temple. "When Jesus had lifted up himself, and saw none but the woman, He said unto her, Woman, where are those thine accusers? Hath no man condemned thee?" The *woman* must have been surprised! No doubt she had trembled with fear. No doubt she wondered if she would be stoned. What surprise she must have felt when Jesus said, "Neither do I condemn thee! Go and sin no more." In other words, Jesus said "Woman, in spite of your adultery, in spite of the scarlet sin you have committed, I came not to condemn — but to save." Jesus saved her.

I do not know what Jesus wrote on the ground the two times He stooped and wrote with His finger; but whatever He wrote was the Word of God, and the Word is the power of God unto salvation (Rom. 1:16). Hearing the Word brings salvation (John 5:24) and the seed of the Word brings the new birth (I Peter 1:23). God's grace saves us — but saving grace becomes our personal possession by faith. Faith comes by hearing, and hearing by the Word of God (Rom. 10:17). Therefore, whatever Jesus wrote on the ground surprised and convicted the Pharisees, and they departed. Whatever He wrote on the ground must have surprised the dear woman exceedingly; but the Scriptures He wrote also brought salvation to her sinful heart. She went away a child of God.

SAUL OF TARSUS. We find the fast moving account of the conversion of Saul of Tarsus in Acts 9:1-19. Saul was a devout Pharisee. He was dedicated — soul, spirit and body — to the religion of the Jews. He persecuted the church in Jerusalem, and when he had done all he could to destroy the believers there, he went to the high priest and asked for letters — we would call them *warrants* — to go into the cities and synagogues in Damascus to arrest the believers and bring them back to Jerusalem.

Just before he reached Damascus, "Suddenly there shined round about him a light from heaven" (Acts 9:3). Saul fell to the earth and lay prostrate on the ground, blinded by the extreme brightness of the heavenly vision. He heard a voice from Heaven saying, "Saul, Saul, why persecutest thou me?" To say that Saul was *surprised* would be an understatement! He was undoubtedly amazed, astonished — perhaps frightened beyond words. When he asked "Who art thou, Lord?" the answer came back, "I am Jesus whom thou persecutest." Trembling in fear and amazement, Saul said, "Lord, *what wilt thou have me to do?*" Then the Lord instructed him to arise and go into the city, where he would be told what he should do.

Saul arose, opened his eyes — but he could not see! The men with him led him into Damascus, "and he was three days without sight, and neither did eat nor drink."

The Lord appeared to Ananias, a believer who lived in Damascus, and gave him instructions concerning Saul. Ananias, who was reluctant to meet Saul, said, "Lord, I have heard by many of this man, how much evil he hath done to the saints at Jerusalem: and here he hath authority from the chief priests to bind all that call on thy name!" (Acts 9:13-14). But the Lord assured Ananias that Saul was a chosen vessel, that he would hear instructions from him, and would become a minister to the Gentiles. "And Ananias went his way, and entered into the house; and putting his hands on him said, Brother Saul, the Lord, even Jesus, that appeared unto thee in the way as thou camest, hath sent me, that thou mightest receive thy sight, and be filled with the Holy Ghost" (Acts 9:17). Saul received the message, his blindness departed, his heart was opened, the Holy Spirit came in. He was baptized, and "straightway he preached Christ in the synagogues, that he is the Son of God" (Acts 9:20).

Yes, Saul of Tarsus was extremely surprised when the bright light from Heaven engulfed him and laid him prostrate on the ground; but thank God, his surprise led to his salvation, and Saul of Tarsus became Paul the preacher, one of the greatest who ever lived.

SURPRISES THAT AWAIT SINNERS

All unbelievers who die and find themselves suddenly in hell will be surprised beyond words. Consider several instances from the Scriptures:

In Matthew 14:1-11 we have the story of Herod, who was ruler when John the Baptist began preaching. John preached against Herod's sin, for which Herod promptly had him arrested and thrown in prison. At Herod's birthday party, the daughter of Herodias danced before him, and her dance so inflamed the passions of the king that he lost control of his senses. With an oath he promised the girl she could have whatever she wanted. Her mother had told her beforehand to ask *for the head of John the Baptist*. The king had him beheaded, and his head placed on a charger and presented to the daughter of Herodias.

I believe God made a special note when John's head rolled from the chopping block. John was not just an ordinary preacher — he was chosen and sent by God to announce the coming of Jesus. The disciples came, took up the body of John, and buried him — "And went and told Jesus" (Matt. 14:12).

Later, when Jesus was teaching and preaching in that area,

Herod was very eager to see Him. He thought this miracle-working Person was John the Baptist, risen from the dead. There were those who admonished Jesus to leave that part of the country quickly, lest Herod kill HIM as he had killed John. But Jesus said, "Go ye, and tell that fox, Behold I cast out devils, and I do cures today and tomorrow, and the third day I shall be perfected" (Luke 13:32). Herod is the only man whom Jesus used the name of an animal to describe.

Later, when Jesus sat in the presence of Herod, we read in Luke 23:6-9, "And as soon as he [Pilate] knew that he [Jesus] belonged unto Herod's jurisdiction, he sent him to Herod, who himself also was at Jerusalem at that time. And when Herod saw Jesus, he was exceeding glad: for he was desirous to see him of a long season, because he had heard many things of him; and he hoped to have seen some miracle done by him. THEN HE [HEROD] QUESTIONED WITH HIM IN MANY WORDS; BUT HE [JESUS] ANSWERED HIM NOTHING!"

Herod spoke many words to Jesus — but Jesus answered not one word. To the king, this silence must have been surprising past all understanding. Herod is in hell today — begging, pleading, and crying for mercy; but not one word has he ever heard to this day, that would give him any comfort or mercy.

Sinner, if you reject Jesus you, too, will be surprised when you stand before God the Father, and hear Him say to the angels: "Bind him hand and foot and take him away, and cast him into outer darkness where there is weeping and wailing and gnashing of teeth!" When you turn to Jesus begging Him to intercede for you, you will be surprised when He answers not a word! Jesus said, "Whosoever therefore shall confess me before men, him will I confess also before my Father which is in heaven; but whosoever shall deny me before men, him will I also deny before my Father which is in heaven (Matt. 10:31-32).

Confess the Lord Jesus Christ NOW. Call on Him NOW — and He will save you. But if you refuse to confess Him before men, if you refuse to call upon Him in this life, He will refuse to confess you before His Heavenly Father.

The judgment will be a place of many surprises, but I believe the group that will be MOST surprised is the group mentioned in Matthew 7:21-23: "Not every one that saith unto me, Lord, Lord, shall enter into the kingdom of heaven; but he that doeth the will of my Father which is in heaven. Many will say to me in that day, Lord, Lord, have we not prophesied in thy name? and in thy name have cast out devils? and in thy name done many wonderful works? And then will I profess unto them, I never knew you: depart from me, ye that work iniquity."

The very fact that they name their good works suggests great surprise. In other words "Lord, you cannot send us to hell. We preached, we cast out demons, we built great churches, we were the head of great religions. You surely will not send US to the pit!" But the Lord Jesus makes it clear that they cannot enter heaven. Why? "I NEVER KNEW YOU!"

This passage does not refer to a group of preachers and church workers who were saved and fell from grace. These dear souls were depending upon their good works to get them into heaven. *There are many doing just that today!* It is not by works of righteousness which we have done, but according to His mercy He hath saved us (Titus 3:5).

Could there be anything worse than going to hell? I think going to hell, when you expect to enter heaven, would be worse. And according to the Words of Jesus in the Sermon on the Mount, there will be many such people. *What a surprise it would be to be consigned to hell* when entrance into heaven is anticipated! Please do not let it happen to you, dear soul. Are you "working and doing," or are you TRUSTING and BE-LIEVING?

SURETIES

SURITIES TO THE BELIEVER. There are many things you and I

may never know, there are many things we may never understand; but there is one thing we can know for sure: "I KNOW WHOM I HAVE BELIEVED" (II Tim. 1:12). We may never understand much about the Bible. There may be more Scriptures that we do not understand, than Scriptures we DO understand; but we can know this:

God so loved the whole world, and gave His only begotten Son, that *whosoever* — regardless of race, creed, color, social standing, wealth, or whatsoever — believeth on Him should not perish, but have everlasting life (John 3:16). We can know that salvation is a gift (Eph. 2:8-9). Even a child understands a gift. There must first be a *giver*, the one who possesses the gift to be given. Then to complete the transaction there must be a *receiver* — and that is where WE come in. God so loved sinners that He gave Jesus — and when we *receive* Jesus He saves us ...and we are sure! (John 1:12).

But HOW are we sure?

a. "If any man have not the Spirit of Christ, he is none of his" (Rom. 8:9).

b. "The Spirit himself beareth witness with our spirit, that we are the children of God" (Rom. 8:16).

Therefore, if we are believers, the Holy Spirit bears witness with our spirit that we are God's children.

Jesus said, "Verily, verily, I say unto you, he that heareth my word, and believeth on him that sent me, hath everlasting life, and shall not come into condemnation; but is passed from death unto life" (John 5:24).

Therefore, if we hear the Word of God, and receive the Christ of God according to the terms of the Word, the Word assures us that we are saved.

"And this is the record (recorded Scriptures) that God hath given to us eternal life, and this life is in his Son. He that hath the Son hath life; and he that hath not the Son of God hath not life. These things have I written unto you that believe on the name of the Son of God; that ye may know that ye have eternal life, and that ye may believe on the name of the Son of God" (I John 5:11-13).

I do not hesitate to say there is no such thing as salvation without assurance. If you are *saved,* you are *sure:*

We can know we are saved through the testimony of our own hearts: "My little children, let us not love in word, neither in tongue; but in deed and in truth. And hereby WE KNOW THAT WE ARE OF THE TRUTH, AND SHALL ASSURE OUR HEARTS BEFORE HIM. For if our heart condemn us, God is greater than our heart, and knoweth all things. BE-LOVED, IF OUR HEART CONDEMN US NOT, THEN HAVE WE CONFIDENCE [assurance,. surety] TOWARD GOD" (I John 3:18-21).

Every believer can be sure that Jesus not only saves; but every believer can be sure that God's grace is sufficient to keep all the way, even to the end. "...for he hath said, I WILL NEVER LEAVE THEE, NOR FORSAKE THEE. So that we may boldly say, The Lord is my helper..." (Heb. 13:5-6).

David, a man after God's own heart, said, "Yea, though I walk through the valley of the shadow of death, I will fear no evil, for thou art with me.... Surely goodness and mercy shall follow me all the days of my life, and I shall dwell in the house of the Lord forever" (Psalm 23:4-6).

Since God is no respecter of persons (Rom. 2:11), the assurance Paul possessed, the assurance John possessed, the assurance David possessed, the assurance saints have always possessed, can be yours and mine. Are you sure your name is in the Lamb's Book of Life?

SURETIES TO THE SINNER. Every unbeliever who reads these lines may rest assured that "All we like sheep have gone astray — but the Lord hath laid on HIM the iniquity of us all" (Isa. 53:6).

"For all have sinned and come short of the glory of God"

(Rom. 3:23). "The wages of sin is death; but the gift of God is eternal life through Jesus Christ our Lord" (Rom. 6:23).

"Except your righteousness shall exceed the righteousness of the scribes and Pharisees, ye shall in no case enter into the kingdom of Heaven" (Matt. 5:20).

"And there shall in no wise enter into it [Heaven] anything that defileth, neither whatsoever worketh abomination, or maketh a lie: but they which are written in the Lamb's book of life" (Rev. 21:27).

"The wicked shall be turned into hell, and all the nations that forget God" (Ps. 9:17).

"And I saw the dead, small and great, stand before God; and the books were opened: and another book was opened, which is the book of life: and the dead were judged out of those things which were written in the books, according to their works. And the sea gave up the dead which were in it; and death and hell delivered up the dead which were in them: and they were judged every man according to their works. And death and hell were cast into the lake of fire. This is the second death. And whosoever was not found written in the book of life was cast into the lake of fire" (Rev. 20:12-15).

My closing word to the unbeliever is simply this: You can be sure that you will not, you cannot, enter Heaven unless you are saved by God's grace, through faith in the shed blood of Jesus; and if you refuse to believe on the Lord Jesus Christ, rest assured that you, like the rich man, will open your eyes in the flames of hell! God help you, dear unbeliever, to receive the Lord Jesus Christ now — and He will SAVE you now! If you are a church member and you doubt your salvation, put your complete faith and confidence in the finished work of Jesus. Do not doubt Him any more. It is a sin to doubt God, for "God cannot lie" (Titus 1:2; Heb. 6:18).

To that precious church member who may have read this message and just "supposes" that everything is all right between you and God, you are a church member, and therefore, you "suppose" you will go to Heaven, you have been baptized and you "suppose" you are a Christian — please do not live one moment longer on *supposition*. Go to the Word of God and search the Scriptures. Believe on the Lord Jesus Christ, and your supposition will be replaced with surety. You can sing "Blessed assurance, Jesus is mine! Oh, what a foretaste of glory divine!"

Jesus came that we might have life, and have it more abundantly (John 10:10). No person can enjoy the abundance of God's grace until he has been truly born again, until he truly rests in Jesus, and until he knows for sure that every sin is under the blood.

To live in supposition concerning your eternal destiny is the most dangerous thing you can do. Life is uncertain — you may die tonight! Then which surprises would you know — those which await the believer as he enters the glories of heaven? or those which await the unbeliever in hell where the fire is not quenched and the worm does not die?

God grant that may never happen to you! May this be the day you make your calling and election sure!